BREW CHEM 101

BREW CHEM 101

Lee W. Janson, Ph.D.

A *Storey Publishing Book*

Storey Communications, Inc.
Schoolhouse Road
Pownal, Vermont 05261

*The mission of Storey Communications is to serve our customers
by publishing practical information that encourages personal independence
in harmony with the environment.*

Edited by Deborah L. Balmuth
Cover design and illustration by Greg Imhoff
Text design by Cindy McFarland
Production assistance by Therese Lenz
Indexed by Northwind Editorial Services

Printed in the United States by Vicks Lithograph & Printing Corp.

10 9 8 7 6 5 4 3 2 1

Library of Congress Cataloging-in-Publication Data

Janson, Lee W., 1964–
    Brew chem 101 : the basics of homebrewing chemistry / Lee W.
Janson.
       p.   cm.
    "A Storey Publishing book."
    Includes bibliographical references (p.) and index.
    ISBN 0-88266-940-0 (pbk. : alk. paper)
    1. Brewing—Amateurs' manuals.   I. Title
TP570.J34   1996
641.8'73—dc20
                                        96-13207
                                           CIP

Contents

Acknowledgments

Numerous people are either directly or indirectly responsible for the writing of this book, all of whom deserve much thanks. Members of both the Bay Area Mashtronauts and Houston Foam Rangers were among the first to hear early versions of this manuscript and their feedback was most helpful. I would particularly like to note the help of Mike Wiley of Wines, Etc., who not only started me on this brewing journey but who has also always been there with advice or encouragement. The staff and management of Tindy's German Restaurant and Bier Garden as well as The Gingerman deserve a great deal of thanks as gracious hosts during my required "research."

I would also like to thank the members of the 1993 BJCP Study Group from which the start of this book arose, especially the organizers Steve and Autumn Moore. The efforts of Scott Birdwell, the BJCP examiner and owner and purveyor of DeFalco's Homebrew Supplies, are also appreciated.

The writings of Charlie Papazian, Fred Eckhardt, Greg Noonan, and others provided not only an educational basis but a literary framework for this book. Especially helpful have been both the encouragement and critical commentary of Dr. George Fix and Dave Miller. I would also like to thank Dr. Grant Mastick, who, as a fellow graduate student, led me into the world of beers beyond "American Standard." Finally, I must thank my family for their constant support, truly the most appreciated gift.

Introduction

Why would anyone care about the chemistry of beer and beer making? Good question. Homebrewing should not necessarily be an academic pursuit. Many homebrewers don't know and really don't care about the exact details of what is happening in their fermenters. But why should they? Using simple sterile techniques and a few easy steps, the average homebrewer creates wonderful beers that put many larger, commercial breweries to shame.

However, an elementary knowledge of the basic chemistry and biochemistry of the components of beer and of fermentation can be invaluable to the homebrewer, whether beginner or expert. Suddenly those strange steps in mashing and fermenting make sense. Suddenly those sterile techniques seem worthwhile. Suddenly those annoying *off flavors* disappear. Suddenly we truly understand what is happening in that golden, amber, brown, or black mix we will soon call our beer. Suddenly (perhaps) that good beer becomes great beer. And the homebrewer actually knows why!

A small number of authors, most notably Dr. George Fix, have written on this topic. Their work appears in books and in many fine articles in homebrewing magazines. But the average homebrewer can be easily lost in the molecules and electrons that are a part of many explanations. So, is it necessary to have an advanced degree to understand the sometimes cryptic writings of brewing chemistry? Certainly not. On a basic level, anyone can learn the necessary details of a yeast cell's life or the careless steps that produce off flavors and how to avoid them.

Brew Chem 101 is written in simple, nonchemical language for the nonchemist, nonbiochemist homebrewers who wish to know what is happening in their homebrew in simple, understandable terms. Although some molecular structures and descriptions are provided for curiosity's sake, detailed explanations have been predominantly left out of any discussions.

In this book, we cover the various ingredients found in beer, explaining how and why they do (and sometimes don't do) what we want them to do. We begin with a simple discussion of the chemistry and biochemistry of beer's major ingredients, and then of the brewing process, including fermentation — arguably the most important reaction in homebrewing. We also review the chemistry of mashing and sparging, and some unappreciated aspects of wort boiling.

With an understanding of basic brewing chemistry, you will be better at identifying the causes of various off flavors and knowing how to avoid them. Chapter 5 of this book provides a comprehensive review of the major and minor off flavors that may be found in beer, an explanation of their sources, and methods for avoiding them. Finally, you will have an opportunity to put your new-found knowledge to the test with a primer on beer drinking and judging. Using this information, you will be able to fully appreciate as well as enjoy the experience of any beer you drink.

So, relax, get a homebrew, and read on.

Note: Terms appearing throughout this book in **_bold italic_** type (such as **_off flavors_** on page 1) are defined in the Glossary on pages 99 to 106.

1. The Basic Chemistry of Brewing

L et's start our discussion by reviewing the basic steps of home-brewing. We'll also go through steps where problems can result if certain simple rules and techniques aren't followed. Now don't worry if this all seems overwhelming or if you don't know some of the names. We'll cover each one in simple, easy terms in upcoming chapters. Remember, we're supposed to be relaxed!

Three Approaches to Homebrewing

First, there are three overall approaches to homebrewing: *extract*, *all-grain*, and extract and grains. Extract is simply a commercially prepared, syrupy mixture of sugars and proteins that, along with added yeast, will produce alcohol and give a lot of the tastes to the finished beer. Different extracts are available that produce differ-ent flavors and, therefore, different styles of beer. The extract brewer uses this prepared mixture to make a very easy, yet still tasty batch of beer. All-grain homebrewers make an equivalent of extract in place of the store-bought versions. All-grain brewing is the most involved method of brewing, but also the cheapest and best for really crafting a personalized batch of homebrew. As a rule, commercial breweries, microbreweries, and brewpubs do all-grain brewing. Homebrewers can also use extract plus selected grains to make the whole brewing process a bit easier, but still maintain a fair amount of control over the tastes and quality of their beer.

Mashing and Sparging

Homebrewers who use grains (all-grain as well as extract/grain brewers) want to get all the good sugars and proteins into their beer but leave a number of unwanted molecules out. This selected extraction process starts with proper preparation of the malted grains by gentle crushing. Once prepared, the all-grain brewer will go through a process called *mashing* and *sparging*. Some of the most prevalent off flavors in commercial and homebrewed beer can come from the all-grain process. Many of these same off flavors can also result when an extract/grain brewer improperly adds their specialty grains. These off flavors are really rather easy to avoid with just a few simple precautions (covered in detail in Chapters 4 and 5).

The Boiling Process

After mashing and sparging, the all-grain brewer is at the same place that the extract and extract/grain brewers start, namely the boil. The boiling process is important for a number of reasons. First is sanitation. Any bacteria or other nasty bugs in the air or liquid can quickly turn our beer into something better poured down the sink than drunk. Boiling for thirty minutes or more ensures that all of these unwanted visitors are killed off.

Besides sanitation, boiling also helps to prepare all the sugars and proteins for proper fermentation, creating a number of the good flavors in beer. However, if this boiling process is improperly performed a number of off flavors can result, ruining what could have been a good batch of beer. Hops are also added during the boil at different times and in selected amounts. This selected addition is what gives a beer its particular hop aromas and tastes. Finally, certain substances that help produce uncloudy beer are added during the boil.

Pitching the Yeast

After the boil comes cooling in preparation for adding or **pitching** the yeast. The final cooled temperature will depend on the type of yeast being used and, to a certain extent, the style of beer being brewed. Perhaps more important than the exact final temperature is the speed at which we cool the liquid, since it is directly related to certain off flavors. Fast cooling also helps remove cloudiness from beer. A number of quick cooling techniques have been developed over the years to get the hot boiling water down to a pitching temperature as fast as possible. After cooling, the homebrewer transfers the liquid concoction to a fermenter. This transfer should be done with some mixing and agitation to give the yeast some oxygen. However, this is the one and only time we want to shake up our beer. Shaking or *oxygenating* the beer at other times will usually result in old, stale tastes.

After cooling and transferring, the yeast are added and they go to work making alcohol as well as producing some of the final flavors in our beer. The health of the yeast and the selection of the particular yeast strain is very important in producing the flavors we want. As a side note, when homebrewers or scientists say *yeast* they usually mean more than one since the majority of time they are using a whole lot more than just one yeast cell, hence the plural verbs following the word yeast. When we're just talking about one yeast cell, it will be obvious. Once our yeast are in the fermenter along with the soon-to-be beer, we want things to start happening. However, there's going to be a slight delay before we start seeing some activity. The yeast are getting prepared and things are settling in for a proper fermentation, a process that can take a number of hours.

Fermentation

When that fermentation starts, though, you'll know it. A good, healthy fermentation is just that — good and healthy. The vigorous release of gas can sometimes be alarming. A slimy brown crud called **krausen** will also often form on the top of the beer. The formation of krausen, which is filled with a bunch of bitter hops oils, is a sign of proper fermentation and is good in its own way, since it helps you get all those bad flavors out of your beer. The vigorous release of gas is also good since it mixes your beer (without adding oxygen) and helps remove a number of off-flavor molecules. After a few days, this strong fermentation will subside and a gentle bubbling will start. When this bubbling gets really slow (about once per 90 to 120 seconds) or if you measure your beer and find out the yeast are through (don't worry about how we do this now), it's time to bottle or keg what is now truly beer. This may also be the time when some homebrewers transfer their beer to another fermenter for additional, advanced brewing techniques and/or aging.

Bottling or Kegging

When the beer is ready for bottling or kegging, the homebrewer cleans and sanitizes the bottles or kegs (to kill off any bacteria), adds a little more sugar to the beer (so the yeast can build up carbonation in the bottle or keg), and then transfers the beer with minimal agitation (remember, we don't want any added oxygen now). Homebrewers who keg sometimes carbonate their beer artificially, so, for them, the extra sugar isn't needed. Once bottled or kegged, a cap or cork is put on and the aging and conditioning process starts. During this period of time the flavors in the beer are blending and maturing, usually taking around two weeks (plus or minus a week) for ales and up to a few months for lagers. After aging and conditioning, the only thing left is to drink the beer, which usually is the easiest part of the brewing process.

OK, fellow brewing chemists, now that we know the basics of making beer, let's find out what's really happening.

A Five-Minute Chemistry Lesson

Before we start talking about the brewing chemistry of beer, we'll have to learn a little bit about the language of chemists and biochemists. But, as promised, you don't need to have ever taken a chemistry class to understand the topics we'll cover. First, we'll learn the "alphabet" of atoms in what is called *organic chemistry*, which is just the chemistry of living things like the barley and hops in beer and, yes, even the humans who drink the beer. Only five letters make up our alphabet — **C**, **O**, **H**, **N**, and **S** — each of which stands for one of the five building blocks of an organic molecule. We'll start with the three most important atoms: C, which stands for carbon; O, which stands for oxygen; and H, which stands for hydrogen.

The Organic Chemistry of Homebrewing

The **carbon** atom is probably the most important one for organic chemists since it is the most basic building block of every living creature. Carbon is actually all around you in various forms — from your bones and muscles to wood smoke from your chimney. (The black soot that used to be a living tree is mostly carbon.)

Oxygen is important to organic chemists for several reasons. First, all living things require oxygen in some form to breathe. Second, oxygen is an important part of water, which is also essential for life. So without oxygen, life as we know it wouldn't exist. Oxygen is also important because it's found in a vast majority of organic molecules, to which it gives some very special chemical qualities.

Where there's either carbon or oxygen, there is usually **hydrogen**. Hydrogen basically plays two roles: First, it helps to "fill out" molecules by binding to spaces left by the other atoms, and, second, it reacts a lot with other molecules. We'll cover both of these ideas in just a minute. But first, there are two more organic atoms that we need to learn about. **Nitrogen**, abbreviated N, is mainly involved in making proteins by helping to string amino acids, the building blocks of proteins, together. **Sulfur**, abbreviated S, can have a very disagreeable smell, identified with rotten eggs, skunks, and other foul-smelling things. We'll see sulfur in — what else? — stinky molecules that can form in beer.

Together, these five atoms — C, O, H, N, and S — can form all the biochemical molecules in beer. Certain parts of these molecules are called *reactive groups*. But, wait. What do we mean

---

CHEMICAL BONDS IN WATER AND ETHANOL

Water

Ethanol

The lines drawn between the carbon, oxygen, and hydrogen atoms represent the bonds.

by "form" molecules, and what are "reactive groups"? You see, these atoms can link to each other to form what are called *chemical bonds*. These bonds have all kinds of fancy chemical qualities like energies and angles, dipolar moments and electron shells and orbitals, but we don't care about that here. The important thing to know is that a C can link or bond to other C's or some O's or H's or any of the other atoms, and vice versa, to make molecules. In chemical notation, these bonds are drawn as lines connecting the two atoms. For example, water is a relatively simple molecule with two hydrogens connected to a center oxygen (see illustration previous page). Ethanol is just two carbons and an oxygen bonded together with some hydrogens taking up the extra spaces.

Six carbon molecules can also link together in a circular form called a *benzene molecule*, as illustrated below. The sides of the circle represent the bonds between the six carbon atoms; nothing more, nothing less. Don't worry about the extra inside lines, which just indicate a double bond. These bonds are continually rotating around the molecules. Sometimes they'll be there and sometimes not, depending on what other atoms bond to the points of the circle.

Now, what about those reactive chemical groups in molecules? Well, if everything is just right, these bonds that we just learned about can break and form a completely new bond between new atoms. If this takes place, we say a "reaction" occurred. The breaking up of sugars and proteins during mashing, oxidation of

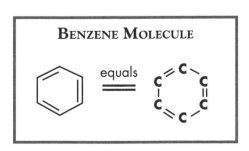

BENZENE MOLECULE

lipids and hop oils, and even the process of fermentation that makes ethanol are all examples of reactions. Reactive chemical groups like C–OH and C=O are where a lot of these chemical reactions take place.

The Inorganic Chemistry of Homebrewing

Now that we've got organic chemistry covered, let's take a brief look at what is called inorganic chemistry, the chemistry of nonliving things. In particular, homebrewers need to understand a group of charged atoms that are collectively referred to as *ions*. Ions are often presented as something mysterious and unknown, but in fact they are simple and help make up many everyday items. Perhaps the best-known ions are sodium and chloride, contained in the salt on your table. Sodium has one positive charge and is abbreviated by chemists as Na^+. Chloride has a negative charge and is written as Cl^-. Much like organic atoms, these two ions bond to form hard, little blocks of $Na^+ Cl^-$, commonly called table salt. (Take a close look at the white things in your saltshaker — all you're looking at is sodium and chloride crystals.) Other ions like calcium (abbreviated Ca^{+2}) and potassium (K^+) are also dissolved in your everyday food. Metals like copper, tin, and zinc can likewise be ions with either positive or negative charges, abbreviated Cu^{+2}, Sn^{+2}, and Zn^{+2}, respectively. When they are ions, these metals join to something with the opposite charge (like $Zn^{+2} Cl^-_2$). The small "2" after the Cl^- indicates that it takes two Cl^- ions to bind with the two positive charges on Zn^{+2}.

The Major Ingredients of Beer

Despite the fact that there are a vast number of styles, substyles, and tastes in beers, the actual ingredients are rather limited. Simply stated, beer is water with alcohol, some grains for flavor, various tastes from flowers of the **hop** plant (much like tea leaves), and a few additional flavors, referred to as **adjuncts**. The infamous *Reinheitsgebot* or German beer purity law of 1516, simply states that only water, malt, hops, and yeast are allowed in beer. (Actually, the law doesn't even mention yeast because their existence wasn't yet known at the time.) Each of the four major ingredients of beer are responsible for a certain defined set of aroma and taste characteristics in your beer. Understanding how and why these tastes come about will make you a better-informed brewer and, as a result, will help you produce higher-quality beers.

Some brewers use a fifth "ingredient" in beer — adjuncts — which opens up an infinite variety of flavor possibilities. Fruits, vegetables, spices, spreads, sauces, small animals, and even large animals have made their way into many a beer recipe, either by choice or by accident. Often the taste is astoundingly good, despite some odd ingredients. However, overuse of adjuncts can lead to less than optimal results. For example, there is a famous American brewer who actually adds the very chemical that causes hangovers. Millions of people drink the beer and unwittingly pay the price for this "adjunct," which is actually an accepted part of the beer's aroma and flavor. In fact, commercial brewers are allowed to add, in any combination, over seventy-five chemicals, dyes, and additives to beer without informing the consumer. This little-known brewing tidbit is why some American microbrewers make a big deal out of the fact that they only use the four basic ingredients and adhere to the mystical German beer purity law. Adjuncts are also briefly covered at the end of this chapter. For more complete sources on adjuncts, see the reading list on page 107.

Water: Role and Importance in Homebrewing

Usually 85 to 95 percent of beer is water. Any flavors (especially off flavors) in the water will come through in the beer.

This is why major brewers often make a point of telling you how clean and pure or special their water is. That's also why you should pay special attention to the quality of your own water. This is harder than it sounds, since water is an extremely complicated molecule. Many very intelligent and skilled people devote their lives to trying to understand "water chemistry," and they still haven't got it all figured out. This doesn't mean it's not worth your time to learn what is known about water and beer. But if you're going to try to do some advanced water manipulations, be forewarned: It's not always as simple as it looks.

THE CHEMICAL NATURE OF WATER. So let's take a quick look at water. We've already seen that water is made of three atoms: one oxygen and two hydrogens. However, when all the chemical bonding and reacting is over, the water molecule is left with partial charges on it — a partial positive charge at each of the hydrogens and a partial negative charge at the oxygen, very much like the electrical charges running through the wires in your house (see the illustration on page 8).

HOW WATER DISSOLVES OTHER MOLECULES. Why should we care about the electrical properties of water? Well, those little charges help to dissolve things. There's a standard rule in chemistry that "like dissolves like," so something with charges dissolves something else with charges. A majority of biochemical molecules have charges or partial charges. For example, table salt, or $Na^+ Cl^-$, dissolves well in water because the ions are charged. Sugars have partial charges so they dissolve, too. Therefore, water, with its partial charges, is a great solvent for many things, including a number of the ingredients you want in your beer.

But what about those things that don't have charges and therefore can't be dissolved easily by water, like many hop oils?

These are often referred to as *hydrophobic* molecules, which literally means "afraid of water." Hydrophobic molecules either need something hydrophobic to dissolve in (remember "like dissolves like") or they need to change to a molecule with some partial charges that can, therefore, dissolve. In brewing, this change is often referred to as *isomerization*, and just involves changing some of the bonds around until some partial charges are formed. (See reading list on page 107 for books on this topic.)

Even after the hydrophobic molecules have isomerized and gained some partial charges, water still may have some trouble dissolving them; this is where the ions come into the picture. The partial charges often just form on certain parts of the molecule and there may be too many "water-fearing" parts of the hydrophobic molecule left. But, just like water, each of the charged ions helps to dissolve things. This process gets admittedly a little complicated, but, depending on their individual chemical properties, certain ions will work with the water and finally get the hydrophobic molecule to go into solution. The particular ion or ions involved depends a lot on what the actual hydrophobic molecule is, concentrations of the ion(s) and hydrophobic molecule, temperature, and a bunch of other fun scientific stuff. We'll leave it at that, but remember that even though this cooperative process is sometimes not perfect, when you put water together with some ions, they can dissolve most things that homebrewers need in their beer. Heat also helps water to dissolve things with and without charges, which is one reason why homebrewers boil their starting ingredients.

Many of these ions also change the amount of acid in the beer **mash** and/or **wort.** These changes can affect the ability of the water and ions to dissolve all the malts, hops, and other goodies that make up beer. Therefore, changing the amount of acid by changing the amount and type of ions can directly affect the beer's composition and flavor. We'll talk a bit more about acid level in Chapter 4 in the information on mashing and sparging, but a detailed discussion of this topic is not needed here. A much more thorough review of water chemistry, flavor, and acid level and the dissolved ions that affect them is given by Dave Miller and Greg Noonan in their books (see reading list on page 109).

Ions Found in Water and Their Effects on Beer Flavor

Ion	Effect

Calcium (Ca^{+2}) At proper levels, required by yeast. Helps to maximize extraction of bitter flavors from hops and assists in clarification, stability, and flavor of beer. In excess, can remove essential yeast nutrients from wort and cause haze.

Carbonate (CO_3^{-2}) At high levels, extracts excessive bitter hops flavor (often masked by heavier beers).

Chloride (Cl^-) Increases bitterness, stability, and clarity of beer. At higher levels, gives pleasant round and full sweetness to beer. Can also inhibit yeast flocculation.

Copper (Cu^{+2}) Can cause unwanted yeast mutation and/or death as well as haze formation. Essential for yeast viability at trace levels.

Fluoride (Fl^-) Causes no known flavor or brewing changes. It helps your teeth and bones, though.

Iodine (I^-) Can be used for checking starch conversion (see Chapter 4) as well as sterilization of brewing supplies. Can give dry, semibitter flavor to beer if in excess or not properly diluted or rinsed.

Iron (Fe^{+2} or Fe^{+3}) Essential at trace levels. Additional iron may inhibit yeast metabolism, cause haze, and give an undesired metallic or "inky" taste to beer.

Lead (Pb^{+2}) Neurological toxin in humans (i.e., causes nerve and brain problems). Also causes haze.

THE ROLE OF IONS. These ions do more than just dissolve the parts of beer, though. Some of them have very definite tastes (just think of how table salt, or $Na^+ Cl^-$, tastes), and those tastes can give very special and characteristic flavors to beer. Therefore, some ions are purposely used to produce certain beer styles. One example is the English Burton Pale Ales, so called because they

ION	EFFECT

Magnesium (Mg^{+2})   Essential for yeast metabolism. In small amounts, increases beer flavor. In excess amounts, gives strong bitter flavor.

Manganese (Mn^{+2})   Trace amounts are essential for proper yeast metabolism. Above trace levels, gives an undesired taste to beer.

Nickel (Ni^{+2})   Gives metallic flavor at any levels above trace.

Nitrate (NO_2^{-2})   Has no effect on beer flavor or yeast health. Can be converted to harmful nitrite by contaminating bacteria (See **Nitrite**).

Nitrite (NO_3^+)   Extremely toxic to yeast even at trace levels.

Potassium (K^+)   Gives salty taste to beer. In excess, can inhibit yeast metabolism.

Silicate (SiO_4^{-4})   Causes no change in flavor. Can cause improper mash filtering and haze. Can also cause hard scaling on brewing equipment.

Sodium (Na^+)   Normal levels increase flavor of beer, giving a "round smoothness." Coupled with sulfate, will give an unpleasant harshness.

Sulfate (SO_4^{-2})   Gives very sharp, dry, full flavor to beer. Coupled with sodium, gives a noticeable harshness.

Tin (Sn^{+2})   Can cause haze and metallic flavors.

Zinc (Zn^{+2})   Essential yeast nutrient at trace levels. Poisonous to yeast at excess levels.

use water from Burton on Trent. The water from this river is very high in a number of ions, including calcium, sulfates, magnesium, sodium, and chloride. The combination of these excess levels of ions in the hands of good brewmasters produces a wonderfully complex and delicious taste. This is why homebrewers who want to make a certain style of beer need to be a bit more concerned about the content of their water.

Finally, just as many ions help beer components react, a number of them also help yeast turn the sugars in beer to ethanol. So, not surprisingly, yeast need certain ions to work correctly. The table on page 15 lists a number of ions that are important to brewing, how each helps dissolve beer components, how they affect aromas and/or flavors, and how they help all of the yeastie-beasties do their job.

WATER — THE BOTTOM LINE. Should you, as a homebrewer, spend a lot of time studying water chemistry, having your water analyzed, and playing with adding and removing ions? Well, if you get into that stuff, then go for it. For the majority of homebrewers, though, the water that comes out of our tap or maybe even bottled water is the answer. But which is better?

The bottom line is if your tap water is good, then it's the cheapest and best thing for your brewing. But, if you know there is something bad in your water, then you probably don't want it in your beer. For example, if you know your water is hard (soap barely foams up; you get deposits around your faucets and drainpipe fittings), then it contains a lot of dissolved ions, metals, and/or minerals that are going to affect your beer. If you know your water is soft (soap really foams; you have a filter that takes almost everything out of the water), then it probably lacks some of the ions that the yeast need to live and your beer needs to taste good. If either of these descriptions sound like your water, then consider using bottled water, which has undergone special purification steps, or purifying tap water yourself with store-bought filters.

If you do use bottled water, realize that there are lots of brands and they all don't taste alike. Find the brand and style you like — and, more importantly, would like in your beer — and stick with it; at least you'll always start with the same water taste. Also, stay away from *deionized* or *distilled* water, which has very few of the ions necessary for making beer and proper fermentation. Stick with *drinking* water (but *not* sodium-free) — it has everything a good beer needs and nothing a good beer *doesn't* need. Now that we've got water under control, let's move to the good stuff: malt and hops.

Malt: Source of Sweet and Specialty Tastes

Malted grains are the major source of sugars and proteins that provide the alcohol, body, and head retention in beer. Certain grains also provide special flavors and smells such as the roastiness in stouts and colors such as deep amber in dopplebocks. Even a red color can be created by using a particular specialty grain called Belgian Special B, developed by the makers of Chimay Red. Thus, malts are one of the major contributors to the characteristic flavors, aromas, and colors of varying styles of beers.

Hops: Source of Bitter Tastes and Nonsugar Aromas

Only the cone-shaped flower clusters of the female hop plant (*Humulus lupus*) — a member of the mulberry family — are of interest to brewers, giving beer its distinctive hops flavors and aromas. More specifically, small yellowish sacks beneath the hop flowers contain the important resins and oils. The male plant doesn't contain any useful resins or oils and is only used sparingly to breed hops since the female plant can reproduce by cuttings all by herself.

Actually, hops were originally used in beer because they are a natural preservative. However, they were also found to impart varying amounts of bitterness and flavors that many people found pleasant. These bitter flavors are extracted and dissolved in the wort during the wort boil. Different types of hops have different amounts of resins and oils, resulting in varying degrees of bitterness and different flavors and aromas. To make the most of these differences, hops varieties have been commercially culti-vated so that brewers can customize their beers by varying the amount and type of hops.

Malts and Their Characteristics

NAME	CHARACTERISTICS AND FLAVORS

Amber Malt   Rather rare British malt. Gives high-quality copper color and "biscuit" flavor.

Barley (2-Row)   Little or no specialty flavor contribution. High amounts of starch and, as a result, a high potential yield of fermentable sugars. Thin husks result in less tannin flavor.

Barley (6-Row)   No specialty flavor contribution. Fewer potential sugars than 2-row. Thick husks can give high amount of tannins.

Black Patent   Toasted at very high temperatures, which eliminates all malt flavors. Gives dark coloring and sharp burnt flavor, espe-cially when used in excess.

British Mild Malt   Specialty malt somewhat similar to pale malts. Kilning at higher temperatures gives a light, "British-style" toasted malt, which produces a golden to amber color.

Chocolate Malt   Heavily roasted malted barley with smooth, nutty, toasted malt flavors.

Three main groups of chemicals in the hops flower that may be responsible for the tastes and aromas: hard resins, soft resins, and essential oils.

HARD RESINS. These are of no concern to brewers, as they play no role in the tastes or aroma of beer.

SOFT RESINS. These include *alpha acids* and *beta acids*, which impart hops bitterness to beer. Alpha acids are the primary and desired bittering agent. They are one of the hop constituents that

NAME	CHARACTERISTICS AND FLAVORS
Crystal Malt ("Caramel" Malt)	Malted barley specially dried to cause sugar crystallization instead of sugar breakdown. Gives increased fullness, head retention, and sweetness. Also gives a gold/copper coloring. Prime example of crystal malt is "Cara-Pils."
Munich Malt	Very highly toasted specialty malt similar to Vienna Malt style. Gives malty, caramel sweetness and deep amber color.
Roasted Barley	Roasted unmalted barley. Dark brown in appearance. Gives roasted, pleasantly bitter flavor, much like coffee beans. Also gives color to beer.
Toasted Barley	Lightly cooked unmalted barley with light-brown appearance. Toasted flavor is much more subdued than roasted barley.
Vienna Malt	Highly toasted specialty malt similar to Munich Malt style. Gives fuller body and amber color.
Wheat	Specialty malt used in wheat and white beer styles. Gives sour or bitter taste but with offsetting fruitiness. High levels of protein in wheat malt gives beer a cloudy appearance.

must change their chemical structure or *isomerize* both to dissolve and to give their bitter flavor. However, if an alpha acid reacts with oxygen in the air or is *oxidized*, it can't be isomerized. This oxidation changes some of the important chemical bonds required for isomerization so the water and ions can't dissolve them. Therefore, old hops that have been exposed to the air for a long time may not be very useful if being employed particularly for their

THREE ALPHA ACIDS FROM HOPS

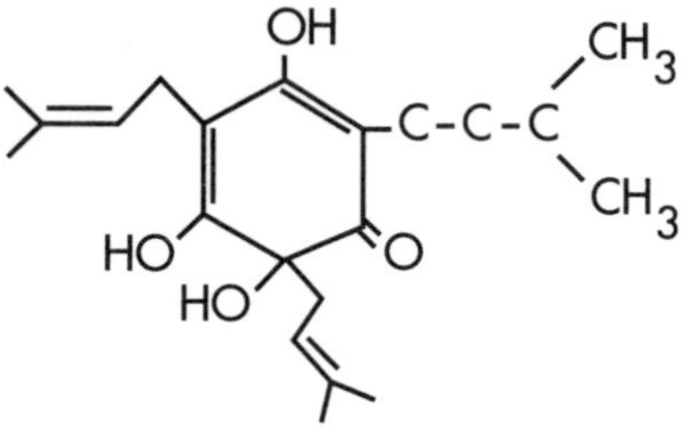

Humulone

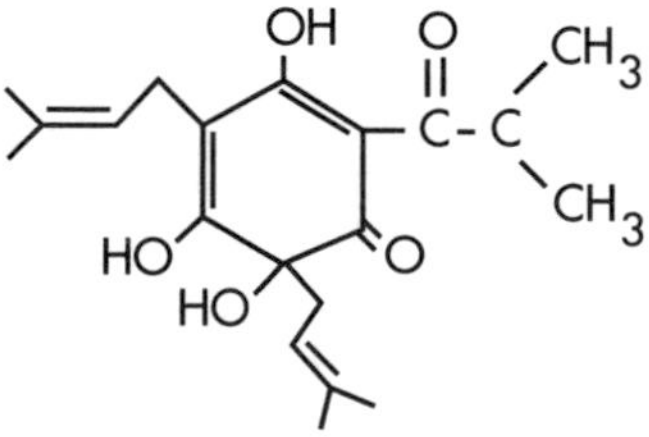

Cohumulone

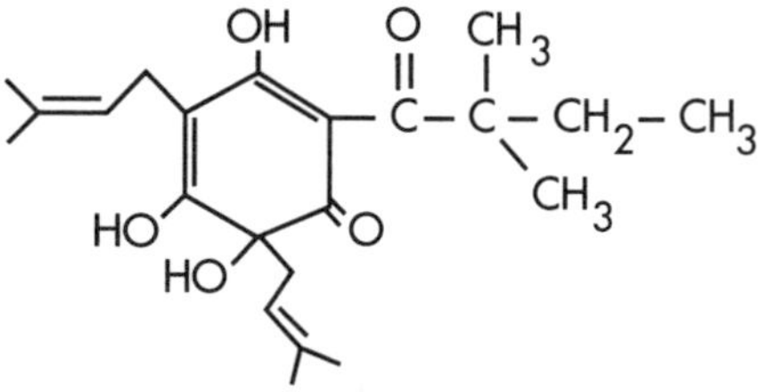

Adhumulone

These alpha acids from hops give the primary and desired bitter flavors to beer. Alpha acids all have the root word "humulone," with or without a prefix.

alpha-acid qualities. Since alpha-acid levels can vary between hop crops, their level is usually noted on the package so the home-brewer can gauge the relative amount of resulting bitterness per ounce of hop added (see **Bittering Units** in Glossary). Alpha acids are found in three different chemical configurations before isomerization, as illustrated on the previous page.

Beta acids don't isomerize; rather, they oxidize to compounds

---

THREE BETA ACIDS FROM HOPS

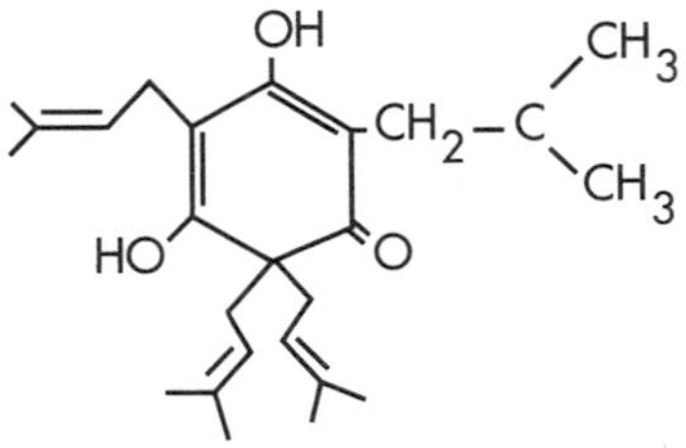

Lupulone

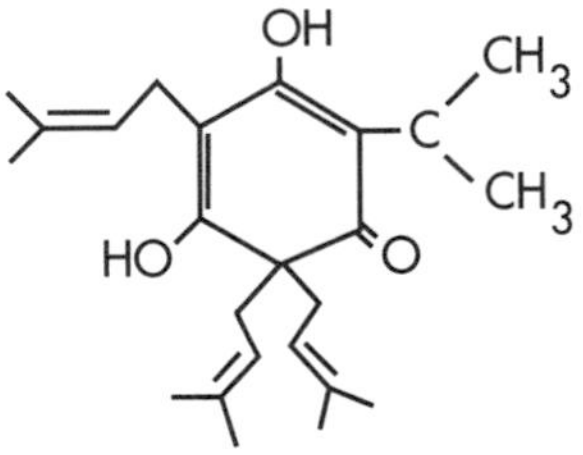

Colupulone

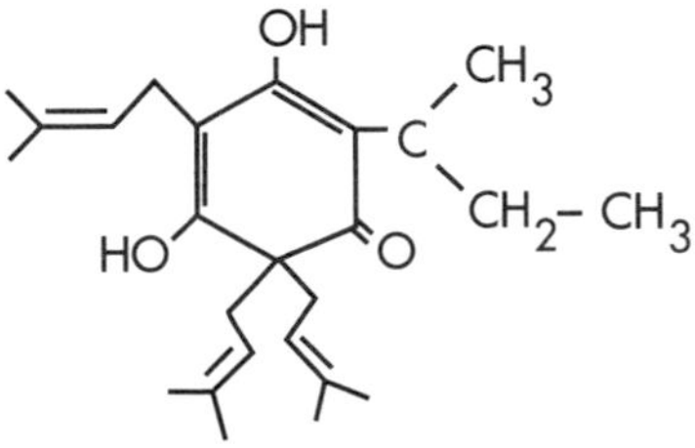

Adlupulone

These beta acids from hops give an undesired bitterness to beer. Beta-acids all have the root word "lupulone," with or without a prefix.

that give their bitterness. However, beta-acid bitterness is usually considered less pleasant than isomerized alpha-acid bitterness. Beta acids are also found in three different chemical configurations (as illustrated on page 21) that are very similar to the alpha acids.

Note that the names of the three major alpha and beta acids are simply taken from the scientific name of the hop plant *Humulus* (alpha acids) *lupulus* (beta acids). Each form either has no prefix (humulone and lupulone), or has the prefix *co*, (cohumulone and colupulone) or *ad* (adhumulone and adlupulone). Cohumulone is the most easily extracted during brewing and, therefore, is often considered the most important soft resin. In fact, the alpha-acid rating of hops is usually just the percentage of cohumulone. **Noble hops** contain low amounts of cohumulone. **High-alpha hops** contain high amounts of cohumulone. These hop varieties are often called **super alphas** to note their high level of bitterness.

ESSENTIAL OILS. There are over two hundred fifty essential oils in the hop flower that contribute the nonbitter flavors and aromas in the plant. The oils that contribute to beer flavor may be divided into four groups based on their chemistry and, in part, their flavor contributions: Hydrocarbons, Oxygenated Essential Oils, Citrus/Piney Essential Oils, and Sulfur-Containing Essential Oils.

Hydrocarbons include mainly *humulene* and *myrcene* (see illustration). Humulene gives beer an elegant, refined taste and aroma. High amounts of humulene are found in the aromatic or so-called noble hops, which include Fuggle, Golding, Hallertau, Hersbruck, Saaz, Spalt, Styrian, and Tettnanger. Myrcene gives beer an intense, pungent taste. Research has shown that the humulene and myrcene oils in hops are normally oxidized or oxygenated (see following section) at a relatively rapid rate even

HYDROCARBONS FROM HOPS

Humulene   Myrcene

These are two important hydrocarbons from hops. Humulene gives an elegant or refined flavor and aroma to beer. Myrcene gives an undesirable pungent taste.

under proper storage conditions. **Dry hopping** actually extracts less oxygenated products than flavoring or aromatic hops boils, leading to increased intensity and stability of the humulene aromatics. Therefore, the flavors and aromas of these hydrocarbons are probably present only when dry hopping is used.

Oxygenated Hop Essential Oils are created when oxygen reacts with both humulene and myrcene. This process is the same as the better-known oxidation process that leads to various types of stale off flavors in beer.

A number of individual oxygenated humulene products can be formed that give floral, haylike, moldy, and/or sagebrush off flavors. However, when several of these molecules are combined, a productive mixing or synergy of flavors appears to cancel out most of the bad flavors and produce some good ones. Oxygenation of other hops constituents actually helps to increase humulene flavor for a few months, but after that their effect lessens quite dramatically.

The oxygenation of myrcene leads to the production of two
molecules — *linalool* and *geraniol* — that impart a floral or herbal
character to beer. Related molecules like *geranyl acetate* and *geranyl
isobutrate* can also form, producing similar results. These oxygenated flavors are generally less pleasant than those from humulene,
tending to have a stronger, less refined character to them, but they
are usually only a problem with hop varieties that have high
amounts of myrcene. One such variety is the widely used Cascade
strain. Beers using this hop are usually marked by a strong floral or
spicy aroma and flavor that is highly prized. However, for beer
styles where such a flavor is unwanted, the use of Cascade hops
and the resulting myrcene flavors could be a problem. See
"Oxidation" on page 75 for more information on oxygenated hop
oil products.

Citrus/Piney Essential Hop Oils can give beer a smell of
citrus fruit or pine. These oils include the *cadinenes*, *citral*, and the
limonenes, among others.

Sulfur-Containing Essential Oils are the source of the off
flavor known as "light struck" or "skunky." Here's our first sulfur
atom, and it's going to smell like — yes — skunk. In fact, similar
molecules are responsible for the notable odor of a skunk.

Yeast: Source of Fermentation (Alcohol Production)

Yeast convert sugars to alcohol by a process that chemists and
biochemists call *anaerobic respiration*, more commonly called
fermentation. Yeast also break down lipids and simple proteins as
they live and grow, which creates many of the final flavors in
beers. Two major types of yeast used in brewing — lager yeast and
ale yeast — can be differentiated by whether they are top or
bottom fermenting, the temperature at which they ferment, and
how well they digest the sugar **raffinose**.

LAGER YEAST. Known by the scientific name *Saccharomyces uvarum* (formerly called *Saccharomyces carlsbergensis* after the Carlsberg brewers and brewery that first isolated the strain), lager yeast gives light, clean aromas and flavors. These yeast are characterized as *"bottom"* fermenting, ferment at cooler temperatures [32 to 55°F (0 to 12.8°C)] and completely digest the sugar *raffinose*.

ALE YEAST. Known by the scientific name *Saccharomyces cerevisiae*, ale yeast give complex, fruity aromas and flavors. Ale yeast are characterized as "top" fermenting, ferment at warmer temperatures [50 to 75°F (10 to 23.9°C)], and don't completely digest the sugar raffinose. A special group of ale yeast that produces high levels of banana and clovelike aromas and flavors is used in the production of wheat-based beers, including Weizen and Weiss styles. This "wheat yeast" has the same three characteristics of ale yeast noted above.

Despite the fact that homebrewers often talk about top, warm-temperature ale yeast and bottom, cold-temperature lager yeast, these definitions are becoming less exact. As new strains of yeast are found, top and bottom start to blend together in a gray zone. For example, some ale yeast settle more to the middle or bottom of the fermenter; some lager yeast float around the middle or even close to the top, so it's hard to say which are staying at the top and which are staying at the bottom. Microbreweries and brewpubs are actually trying to isolate top-fermenting strains that settle to the bottom of fermentation vessels at the end of fermentation, thereby producing clear beer with less work. Temperature constraints are also easing. Some special strains of lager yeast do quite nicely at what have been thought of as ale fermentation temperatures, and a few hearty ale yeast strains can ferment fairly well at temperatures less than 55°F (12.8°C). So the neat categories that homebrewers have developed for yeast, while still intact, are starting to fray at the edges. About the only definite way to tell a lager yeast from an ale yeast is the raffinose test. As discussed on pages 30 to 31, processing of the sugar raffinose is not a major part of fermentation, but it is a nice, exact biochemical test for the type of yeast you have. Yeast are also discussed in more detail in Chapter 3.

Adjuncts: Source of Specialty Tastes Not Associated with Malts or Hops

Special flavoring ingredients and chemicals, including fruits, honey, and spices, are as varied as the imagination of the homebrewer. Many examples and their particular flavor characteristics are covered in Papazian's *New Complete Joy of Homebrewing.* Off flavors from some adjuncts are covered in Chapter 5.

2. The Biochemistry of Beer

The major components of beer produce three major biochemical classes of molecules: sugars, proteins, and lipids. These three major ingredients come mainly from malted grains and provide the yeast with a source of food to both live on and, as a fortunate byproduct, from which to create the flavors and aromas of beer. We'll talk more about how yeast do this in Chapter 3. Some of the lipids also come from hops, but these are mainly flavoring oils and really aren't used by the yeast. Whether you are a beginner or expert brewer understanding where each of these major classes of molecules come from (discussed in Chapter 1), what tastes and aromas they provide (described in this chapter), and how they can lead to off flavors (covered in Chapters 4 and 5) will help you maximize your brewing skill and dramatically improve your beer. So, without any further delay, let's continue our discussion.

The Contribution of Sugars (Carbohydrates)

Sugars from the malted grains provide both sweet tastes and nutrients for yeast and are the precursor for alcohol. They are often referred to as carbohydrates by chemists and biochemists. The atoms in sugars can combine to make a number of structures, but for our purposes, we only need to understand two simple sugar molecules — glucose and fructose — and a couple of more complex sugars made by connecting glucoses and/or fructose in various ways. The chemical structure of glucose and fructose molecules are illustrated. It's not essential that homebrewers understand these thoroughly, so we'll use G to refer to glucose and F for fructose.

Glucose

Glucose (G) molecules can combine in chains of varying length to create different complex sugars. These G-derived sugars are actually the main source of food for the yeast in beer. However,

TWO SIMPLE SUGAR MOLECULES

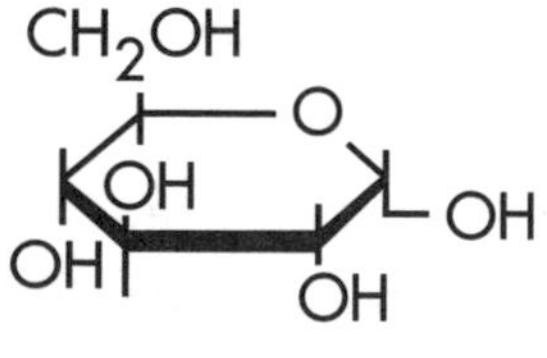

Glucose

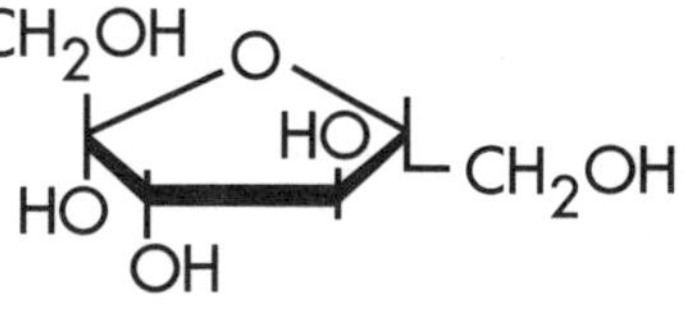

Fructose

These are three-dimensional projections of the glucose and fructose molecules which make up the major sugar types in beer, either individually or in combinations.

only sugar molecules with one, two, or three G's are important for fermentation. Larger sugar molecules (*starch*, *amylose*, and *amylopectin*) are also broken down to these smaller sugars during the processes of mashing and wort boiling, which we'll talk about in Chapter 4. The table below summarizes the major types of glucose-derived sugars, their structures, and the amount of each type found in unfermented beer, also known as *wort*.

Amylopectin and starch have different G to G linkages than amylose or the simpler sugars. These "vertical" linkages can vary in position, creating a large variety of sugar molecules, and aren't broken down by normal brewer's yeast. Therefore, parts of amylopectin and starch molecules remain in the wort and in the finished beer, along with any amylose that isn't broken down to glucose, maltose, or maltotriose during mashing or wort boiling. Since a majority of the smaller sugar molecules will be fermented

Glucose-Derived Sugars Found in the Wort

NAME	NUMBER OF GLUCOSE MOLECULES	STRUCTURE	PERCENT OF SUGAR
Glucose	1	G	8–10
Maltose	2	G	46–50
Maltotriose	3	G — G — G	12–18
Amylose	4 to ~ 1000	G — G — G — ...	Broken down to simpler sugars during malting and mashing
Amylopectin and Starch	4 to 25 25 to ≥ 1000	... — G — G ... G — G — G — G ...	25–35

Note: The general term "starch" is often used (albeit incorrectly) to mean all larger sugars, including amylose, amylopectin, and true starch.

by the yeast, these remaining large sugar parts are mainly responsible for the sweet, so-called malty tastes in beer. One exception is
light beers; for this style, special enzymes are used that break down
many of the complex sugars, thereby allowing them to ferment to
ethanol (which has significantly fewer calories than the original
sugar) and carbon dioxide.

Fructose

Fructose (F) is the other simple sugar that can combine with
itself or with G to make another set of complex sugars that are
important in brewing. These include fructose, sucrose, and
raffinose (see table below).

Raffinose, while not a major component of the wort, is an
important sugar to know as a way to tell the difference between
lager and ale yeasts. Lager yeast can split raffinose into two G's and
one F. The F can, of course, be fermented as normal by either lager
or ale yeast. However, the residual G to G sugar, known as
melibiose, has a slightly different chemical bond than the G to G
bond of maltose (see table on page 29). Lager yeast can split this

Glucose (G)/Fructose (F) Sugars Found in Wort

Name	Number of G and F Molecules	Structure	Percent of Sugar
Fructose	1 F	F	1–2
Sucrose	1 G / 1 F	G — F	4–8
Raffinose	2 G / 1 F	G — G — F	0

Note: Chains of two or more fructose molecules are normally not found since nature
likes to change F to G and then make chains.

bond, giving lager beers a cleaner taste and lighter body. Ale yeast is unable to split this bond. Therefore, a raffinose molecule or a raffinose-like bond between two G's wouldn't be completely processed by ale yeast, leaving a residual sugar and its associated tastes in the final beer. These residual tastes are part of the reason for the more complex flavor and aroma profile of ale-style beers.

Other Complex Sugars

Two other types of complex sugars are also of some concern to the brewer, although not for fermentation. The first, beta-glycans, are closely related relatives of maltose, maltotriose, and the amyloses. The second type, pentosans, are closely related to G and F molecules. However, yeast can't process them like their sugar cousins. If not properly degraded during the malting and mashing process, both beta-glycans and pentosans will cause problems with haze and filtration.

The Contribution of Proteins

Proteins are long strings of individual molecules called *amino acids*. They are required by every living thing from the lowliest bacteria to humans. During the normal brewing process, proteins

---

PROTEIN STRING OF AMINO ACIDS (AA)

AA — AA — AA — AA — AA — AA — AA · · ·

A protein string of amino acids (AA) can be a few AA to several hundred AA long. The length determines the size and molecular weight of the proteins. Individual AA can also be found in beer.

are extracted almost exclusively from the grains.

Many of these proteins are used by the yeast to live, reproduce, and ferment. Proteins used in brewing are classified in one of the following categories:

* **Essential:** Required by yeast for growth and active fermentation.
* **Important:** Necessary for normal yeast growth and fermentation. Yeast can substitute or do without, but beer taste will probably be affected.
* **Nonessential:** Not necessary for yeast growth and fermentation, or proteins the yeast can make themselves.

A majority of proteins in unmalted grains are extremely large. As with sugars, the brewing process removes these large proteins or progressively breaks them down into a size that is usable by the yeast. For example, large proteins are broken down during malting by the heating process. They are also broken down by the action of activated enzymes during mashing, but, even more importantly, many clump together and fall out of the beer. This process is known as *protein precipitation,* or, in brewers' terms, a *break*. Boiling the wort continues the process both by breaking down proteins into shorter and shorter strings of amino acids (through heat) and by changing their natural structure or *denaturing* them, causing a protein precipitation called a **hot break** (much like the whites of an egg cloud up while cooking). Cooling the wort causes another protein precipitation, called a **cold break**. Fast, efficient cooling of your wort can produce a better cold break and dramatically reduce haze in the final product.

During fermentation and aging, the yeast use mainly amino acids and some very small proteins for food. Non-essential, large, and excess proteins are not used by the yeast. Some of these proteins continue to precipitate during wort cooling and fermentation (a less efficient continuation of the cold break), but most are passed to the beer unaltered. The remaining proteins and amino acids give beer much of the body and special flavors characteristic of a certain style and also contribute to head retention. These remaining proteins can be categorized in the following three ways, depending on how long they are and, therefore, how much they weigh:

* **High–Molecular Weight Proteins:** Contribute to body and head retention. Also responsible for chill haze and permanent haze.
* **Medium–Molecular Weight Proteins:** Contribute to body and head retention. Responsible for much of the protein taste in a properly brewed beer.
* **Low–Molecular Weight Proteins and Individual Amino Acids:** Provide nutrients for yeast. Contribute some to protein taste.

The Contribution of Lipids

Lipids, for the purposes of this discussion, are fatlike molecules that come from three sources: malt, oxidized hops, and yeast metabolism. The wort *trub* (pronounced *troob*) — that whitish stuff that collects on the bottom of your fermenter — can consist of as much as fifty percent lipids. Cloudy wort contains from five to forty times the lipid content of clear wort. So what do lipids do, anyway? For the homebrewer they offer two benefits and two drawbacks.

Benefits and Drawbacks

Lipids contribute to yeast viability by transporting nutrients across the yeast's cell wall and cell membrane. Said more simply, they enable yeast to get food. In addition, they inhibit the formation of some unpleasant esters (see page 68 to 69).

One of the drawbacks of lipids is that they decrease head retention by acting like soap and almost literally dissolving the foamy head. They also play an important role in beer staling since they are easily oxidized (see page 76). Oxidized lipids contribute a "soapy," "fatty," "sweaty," or "goaty" taste to old, stale beer.

Because lipids have both strong benefits and drawbacks, the best way to treat them in beer is still somewhat controversial. Some feel a positive contribution from lipids can best occur by transferring the fermenting wort to a second fermenter after a few days, when the initial stages of fermentation are complete. This allows the yeast access to lipids during the critical starting stages of fermentation, but then removes the wort from the high-lipid trub that collects on the bottom of the fermenter. However, different yeast strains produce dramatically different amounts and types of lipids. This varying lipid mixture actually adds specific tastes to and helps define a style of beer. So if you separate the beer from the lipids, you've potentially lost some of the tastes.

Perhaps the best suggestion is found in the *New Complete Joy of Homebrewing:* Homebrewers should rack their beer to a lipid-free secondary fermenter if it's going to sit on the trub for two weeks or more. This method makes sense since all the good contributions from the lipids are going to be over by two weeks; your fermentation should be finished with all the lipid flavors intact and the esters reduced, and you'll either bottle or keg it, eliminating a vast majority of the trub in the process. Of course, some recipes and brewing techniques (such as lagers) require racking to a secondary fermenter, anyway. How about the bad parts of the high-lipid trub? Well, if you think that the only thing that's making or breaking you on head retention is some lipids, you should probably revise your recipe or your brewing technique. Contaminants like soap or bacteria are more likely to be your problem than the trub. Likewise, serious oxidation occurs after two weeks only if your technique is poor, not just because you have beer on the trub.

3. Yeast and Fermentation

Yeast fungus cells are incredible little creatures that eat, drink, and create waste just like other organisms. Fortunately, they like to eat and drink the sugars, proteins, and water in the wort, and the waste they produce is alcohol. This process is called *fermentation*, a term almost always referring only to the anaerobic (without oxygen) processing of sugars. There are thousands of different strains of yeast, each eating, drinking, and excreting waste a little differently. These different strains account for the wide range of flavors in beers, as they produce different levels of esters, diacetyl, and specialty flavors (such as clove in wheat beers).

Characterizing Yeast

As discussed in Chapter 1, yeast used for brewing are classified as either lager or ale (including wheat) yeast. Beyond these general classifications, different strains of yeast can be distinguished by their flavor characteristics (including aromas and flavors), how well they grow and multiply, how well they stay afloat or sink to the bottom of the fermenter (called *flocculation*), and how well they convert the wort sugars into ethanol (called *attenuation*).

Advanced brewers sometimes use other, more complex measures of yeast activity. A short but good review of several yeast strains is given by *Dave Miller's Homebrewing Guide* (see reading list on page 109). More detailed information can be obtained from fellow brewers, from your homebrew supply shop, and by computer on homebrew electronic bulletin boards.

Stages of Yeast Activity in Fermentation

After the yeast are added to, or *pitched*, into the cooled wort, they go through three separate processes leading up to, and including, fermentation.

THE INITIAL PREPARATION PERIOD is essentially a "waking up" and "checking out" period for yeast that have often been dried, processed, packaged, and/or shipped across the country. The waking up phase involves cell-wall preparation, nitrogen uptake, sugar uptake, and oxygen uptake. In other words, the yeast utilize the wort to get themselves in shape for fermentation. A wort that is missing required sugars, proteins, lipids, or ions at this stage will slow or halt the preparation of the yeast.

Even if the yeast are healthy and already actively growing, they will still have to consider, or check out, the new growth environment before committing to it. A yeast colony will not want to put its valuable biological resources into a potentially poor home, so a quick check of food and space is as essential to a yeast cell as it is to any living organism.

The length of time required for all of this preparation is directly related to how healthy the yeast are. Sick or weak yeast won't be prepared as fast as healthy yeast. Dried yeast that come straight out of a packet will take longer to recover than a liquid culture of yeast already growing in a food-filled media. However, even actively growing yeast will still go through a "pitching shock" lag as they check out and get used to their new home.

AEROBIC (WITH OXYGEN) RESPIRATION is the second stage of yeast activity. Yeast cells can get fifteen times more energy from a sugar molecule if they use oxygen. Therefore, while oxygen is available in the wort, yeast will feed using aerobic respiration. The energy produced will help yeast grow and multiply. This is why you want to aerate your wort at the beginning — to get lots of healthy yeast cells before anaerobic fermentation starts. Aerobic respiration produces six molecules of carbon dioxide (CO_2) per sugar molecule metabolized, so you'll start to see bubbles form, despite the fact that alcohol is not being produced. Assuming you have healthy yeast, the time spent in the aerobic respiration phase is directly related to how much dissolved oxygen is in the wort.

ANAEROBIC (WITHOUT OXYGEN) FERMENTATION is the much-awaited final stage of yeast activity. During this time, significant yeast growth and cell division still occur, increasing the number of yeast cells. Since all the oxygen is gone, the yeast cells turn to anaerobic respiration, which leads to ethanol production. One molecule of CO_2 is produced for each ethanol molecule produced (see illustration on page 40). Note the molecule called acetylaldehyde that occurs just before ethanol. We'll talk about it again in Chapter 5 in the discussion of off flavors.

OUTLINE OF THE FERMENTATION PROCESS

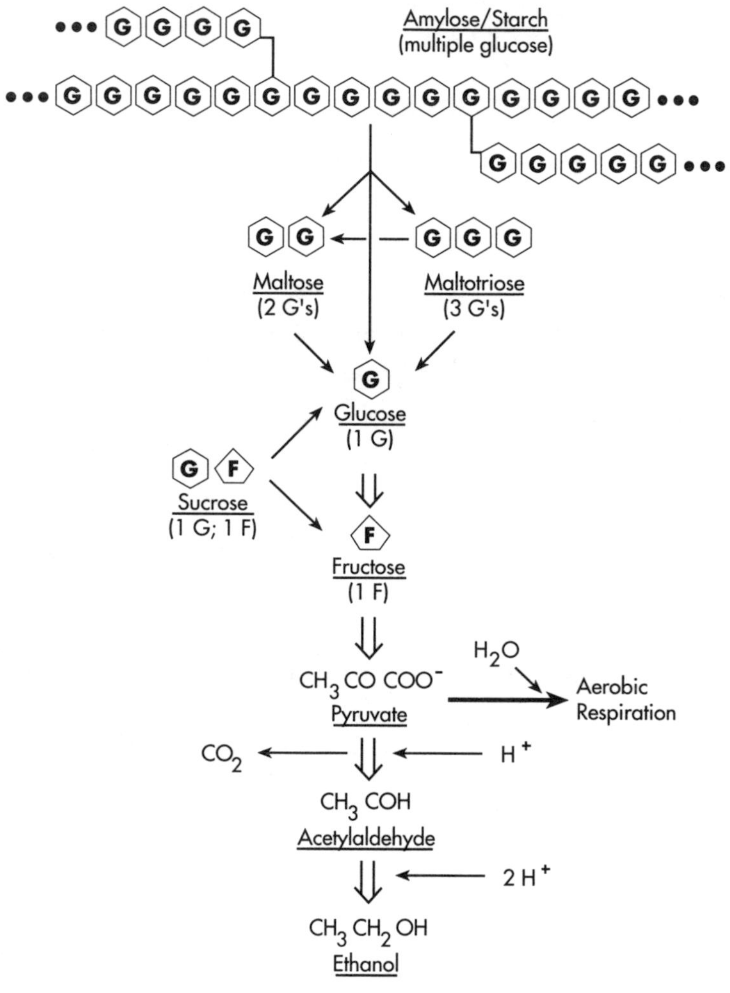

Amylose/Starch
(multiple glucose)

Maltose
(2 G's)

Maltotriose
(3 G's)

Glucose
(1 G)

Sucrose
(1 G; 1 F)

Fructose
(1 F)

$CH_3 CO COO^-$
Pyruvate

H_2O → Aerobic Respiration

CO_2 ← H^+

$CH_3 COH$
Acetylaldehyde

← $2 H^+$

$CH_3 CH_2 OH$
Ethanol

Mashing and wort boiling break down large, complex sugars (amylose/starch) to simpler sugars (maltose, maltotriose, sucrose, glucose, and fructose). Yeast use these simple sugars either by aerobic or anaerobic respiration. Aerobic respiration occurs first while oxygen is present in the wort and results mainly in yeast replication and growth. Anaerobic respiration, also known as fermentation, begins when oxygen is depleted and produces the ethanol and carbon dioxide in beer. See text in this chapter for more details.

4. Mashing and Sparging

As discussed in the preceding chapters, yeast are not able to process most of the various proteins and sugars found in fresh grains. For fermentation to occur, enzymes and heat must be used to break large molecules down into smaller ones that the yeast can use. This breakdown is accomplished in three separate stages of the brewing process: *germination*, *mashing* and *sparging*, and *wort boiling*.

The Germination Process

Germination is the natural preparation of a seed for sprouting, a process involving limited breakdown of sugars in the grain seed to provide food for the young plant. Large grain companies that sell grains for homebrewing almost always perform this process. Since it's the rare homebrewer, indeed, who germinates his or her own grains, we won't say anything more about it.

The Mashing and Sparging Process

Many homebrewers enjoy mashing and sparging to produce essentially the same product that can also be purchased ready-made at a homebrew supply store. Although, at first glance, the process is somewhat lengthy and involved, mashing enables the homebrewer to customize and carefully control the ingredients of a brew (something partly given up by brewers using store-bought extract). The process of mashing and sparging is actually relatively simple and can be broken down into six basic procedures. Although it may seem like a lot of steps to do and a lot of particulars to remember, the overriding purpose is quite straightforward: optimizing the conditions for breaking down the sugars and proteins in grains. The following review is not intended to be an instructional lesson on how to mash, only an explanation of what each step is supposed to do. If you're interested in learning how to mash, I would encourage careful study of Dave Miller's book (see page 109), or talk to your favorite trustworthy and experienced all-grain homebrewer.

Mash-In (Sometimes called Dough-in)

Mash-in is the process of mixing crushed grains (called **grist**) with water at the proper temperature — 95°F (35°C), 122 to 131°F (50 to 55°C), or 150°F (65.6°C). The difference in temperature depends on the type of grain. Different grains must be processed slightly differently to optimize their conversion into fermentable sugars and break down the proteins. This has to do with modification of the grains during germination, **enzyme** levels, and some other complicated reasons, which you don't need to know at this level. The bottom line is that each beer recipe, and, in particular, the grains used in that recipe, will require one or more of the following: an *acid rest*, which works best around 95°F

(35°C); although this practice is used less and less, (as discussed later); a *protein rest*, which works best right around 125°F (51.7°C) plus or minus a few degrees; and, always, a *starch conversion*, which is optimal at 150°F (65.6°C). Therefore, the all-grain brewer determines the best temperature to mash-in based on their recipe and which of these processes they have to perform.

Acid Rest

Before defining *acid rest*, we need to define *acid level*. Acid level simply describes how acidic or basic something is, as measured in units of *pH* that range from 1 to 14. Any pH below 7 is considered acidic and the closer the pH is to 1, the more acidic the sample. For example, water is usually a neutral pH 7, juice from an orange or grapefruit (which contains citric acid) is about pH 3 to 4, vinegar (also known as acetic acid) is about pH 2 to 3, and hydrochloric acid is around pH 1. Any pH above 7 is considered basic, and the closer you get to 14, the more basic the sample. Common examples of bases, which are often used as cleaners, include borax at pH 9, ammonia at pH 10 to 11, and lime at about pH 12.

How is pH measured? Fortunately for us, scientists have developed a simple test using chemicals that change color in response to the pH level. Small strips of *pH paper*, coated with these chemicals, are available in homebrew shops. All you have to do is to put a cooled drop of your mash mixture on the strip of pH paper and compare the resulting color to a reference chart showing the corresponding pH. For high-tech brewers, there are digital pH meters available that can be dipped in the mash, and the pH level magically appears on a display screen.

Now let's go back to the acid rest. The enzymes in the mash that create fermentable sugars and break down the proteins work best at a slightly acidic pH level, between 5.0 to 5.7 (5.1 to 5.3 is optimal). When certain types of malts are mashed in, the resulting mash has too basic a pH. Fortunately, an *enzyme* in the mash called *phytase* can lower, or acidify the pH when given a rest period, hence the term acid rest. The acid rest is best done at 95°F (35°C), the temperature at which phytase is most effective.

The acid-rest method for acidifying the pH has been replaced, to some extent, by an easier and quicker method — the addition of calcium sulfate or calcium chloride — that changes pH by a chemical method we won't go into here. This technique was originally used only for amber or dark malts because people believed it didn't work as well on light or pale beers. However, many mashers have started using it for all beer styles with results equal to the older acid-rest method. As a result, the acid rest is sometimes skipped, in which case the *mash-in process* starts at 122 to 131°F (50 to 55°C).

Protein Rest

A lot of medium– and high–molecular weight proteins are present in the mash at this point after the mash-in and/or acid rest. The actual amount depends on the grains used in a beer recipe. To cut down on chill haze from high–molecular weight proteins and/or to get the lighter, cleaner taste of a lager, enzymes in the mash have to be allowed to break down these proteins. The all-grain brewer, therefore, uses a "protein rest" that offers these enzymes a chance to work at their optimum temperature of 122 to 131°F (50 to 55°C) and pH of 5.0 to 5.5 (obtained during the acid rest) for about 30 minutes. Ales don't usually need a protein rest because the body produced by the extra protein is desired. The wort boil, discussed later in this chapter, also breaks down many proteins in lagers as well as in ales.

Starch Conversion

Mashing for all beer styles from the lightest lager to the darkest ale has to include a starch conversion. This is the most important part of mashing, when many of the large starch, amylopectin, and amylose molecules are broken down to glucose, fructose, maltotriose, and other fermentable sugars, as discussed on pages 28 to 31. The larger molecules that aren't broken down give the beer its sweetness and, to a certain degree, body. Just as with the protein rest, the enzymes responsible for starch conversion have an optimal temperature and pH.

The complicated part of starch conversion is that a number of different enzymes are involved, each having its own optimal conditions. The best temperature and pH for one enzyme limits the effectiveness of one or more of the others and in one case will even destroy one of the other enzymes. Therefore, the most desirable starch conversion temperature/pH is a compromise of what's best for the enzymes as a whole. This compromise condition is 149 to 160°F (65 to 71.1°C) and pH 5.3 to 5.4.

The temperature range is obviously rather broad. However, the specifics of the style of beer being brewed will determine more exact limits of this temperature range since each kind of beer needs to have a starch conversion appropriate for the style. Still, the final choice of temperature within these limits allows the individual brewer to personalize each beer. The exact temperature chosen will help determine the sweetness or dryness of the beer by determining how well the complex sugars are broken down (to be used by the yeast) or left in the wort (to contribute to flavor and body). Making this final choice is discussed in the books of Dave Miller and Greg Noonan (see page 109).

THE IODINE TEST. During the starch conversion stage of mashing, the *iodine test* (or *iodine-starch conversion test*) is performed, a chemical test that tells just how well the larger sugars have been broken down to smaller, fermentable sugars. But, how and why does the iodine test work?

Iodine in solution is yellow. However, if iodine comes into contact with a long, linear starch molecule such as amylose (see table on page 29), the iodine molecule fits into spaces within the starch molecule. The solution turns dark blue (or black if there's enough starch). If the starch has been partially broken down or if it has a lot of branches as with large starch molecules or amylopectin, the iodine and starch molecules won't fit together as well, and the solution will turn a reddish color. If no starch, amylose, or amylopectin are left to combine with the iodine, the solution will remain yellow.

Using this test, the all-grain brewer can easily determine how much breakdown of the mash has taken place. For example, a mash solution that is barely broken down will produce a black iodine test, partial breakdown will result in a red iodine test, and full breakdown to fermentable sugars and a few medium-sized sugars will result in the solution remaining the same yellow color. Intermediate shades of these colors are also possible, indicating that the degree of starch and sugar breakdown is somewhere in between the three examples. But beware: grain husks can also react with iodine and produce a black solution, even when all the sugars have been converted. So, the iodine test has to be conducted very carefully (be sure to get only clear mash liquid with no floating pieces of husk) and interpreted correctly.

Mash-Out

By the time the proteins have been broken down by any protein rest and the large sugar molecules have been broken down to fermentable sugars, you're almost ready to *sparge* and recover all of those freshly prepared ingredients you want in your fermenting beer. But first there is one more step in the mash process killing all the enzymes that up till now you've been so nice to. This mash-out process is accomplished by heating the mash to 168°F (75.6°C). This also helps sparging since the sugary solution will flow better hot (just like heating up syrup for your pancakes in the morning). However, don't go any higher than this temperature or you'll start to pull out husk tannins from the grains or cause some of the larger sugars to reabsorb into your liquid mash. If either happens, astringency and haze may result (see pages 61 to 63 and 71 to 72).

Sparging

Sparging is done by just running water through the mashed grains and collecting the good wort for which you've been working so long and so hard. However, this simple operation can easily create off flavors and other problems if some basic rules aren't followed. By far, the worst problem encountered by the beginning or unknowing sparger is the extraction of tannins, silicates, large proteins, and fatty materials from the grains. Another potential problem is that large starch molecules will redissolve into the liquid wort. These mistakes will result in astringent off flavors and cloudy, hazy beer.

The major causes of these problems are the use of too much sparge water at too high a temperature and too high a pH, the exact conditions that extract all the bad things from the husks. The best way to counter these problems is to follow the advice of Dave Miller: adjust and keep the temperature of your sparge water at 168°F (75.6°C) or lower [as low as 160°F (71.1°C); erring on the low side is better] and the pH at 5.7 (or 6.5 for some dark beers). If you pay close attention to these two factors, you can achieve optimum sparging and avoid any of the problems.

The Wort Boiling Process

At this point in the process, the all-grain brewer and extract brewer are back on the same track, and it's time to boil up all the goodies, including the hops, specialty grains, and any adjuncts. Despite the simplicity of boiling, many important things take place during this step that affect your homebrew. We'll cover them all, one step at a time.

The Role of Boiling Time

Boiling is often not considered important by beginning homebrewers since homebrew kit instructions often make it seem more a passing nuisance than a significant brewing activity. However, wort boiling is important because this is when a number of flavors and aromas are produced, off flavors are driven off, and characteristics of a beer are defined in ways that no other process can recreate.

The exact amount of time for boiling depends on what brewing method the homebrewer is using (extract, extract/specialty-grain, or all-grain) and what the homebrewer may be adding or attempting to achieve during the wort boil. The minimum boiling time, usually agreed to be 30 minutes, should probably only be used by the all-extract brewer. Thirty minutes of boiling insures sterilization and a decent, but not optimal, hot break (precipitation of proteins and phenols during wort boiling), as well as evaporation of diacetyl, dimethyl sulfide, and harsh hop oils that may contribute to their associated off flavors. One hour of rigorous boiling is far better for all extract methods, including that of extract/specialty-grain brewers, since this will insure that all these processes are complete. This also offers a perfect time for adding hops, as discussed on page 52.

All-grain brewers, having just completed mashing and
sparging, go directly into a wort boil for 1 to 2 hours or more. In
addition to the benefits just discussed, the boil destroys any
enzymes that may have survived the mash-out process and
decreases the large volume of wort obtained from sparging to more
manageable levels.

CARMELIZATION. Longer boiling times can be used in a unique
way by the inventive homebrewer. After about an hour of boiling,
concentrated malt undergoes a carmelization process, cooking the
sugars rather than just breaking them down. Scientifically, the
glucoses, fructoses, and maltoses change to simpler carbon
structures that are darker in color. The process is comparable to
making toast in the morning when, in essence, you caramelize the
sugars in the bread, and, as a result, they turn brown. Manufacturers of malt extract use caramelization to produce light, amber, and
dark mixtures. This is also the basic process that grains like amber
malt and black patent undergo when they change color. So if you
want to add a little extra color to your brew, or if you want to
create color using only light grains, boil your brew longer. It's
reported that Paulaner makes Salvator Dopple Bock with all light
grains that are caramelized to produce the characteristic deep
amber, copper color.

Carmelization does have its drawbacks. First of all, the flavor
of caramelized wort is reportedly not as favorable as that produced
by carmelization of grains by the manufacturers or rare
homebrewer. This may be due to the difficulty of caramelizing wort
correctly. Just as you can easily burn your morning toast,
carmelization in the brewing process can easily lead to burning.
Even a little bit of burnt wort can give the whole batch of beer a
bad flavor. To caramelize correctly, you must have excellent
control of temperature and evenly distributed heat throughout the

wort (especially at the bottom of the boiling pot). Too much heat or heat in just one place for even a short time can lead to simple burning, which can ruin a good batch of wort that is so close to becoming good beer. Mix the wort well during boiling to help avoid this problem. The concentration of sugars also affects carmelization, so the type and amount of grains, the amount of sugars you got from the grains, and the amount of water you're using can be factors in your success. As you can see, carmelization can be an involved and tricky process, but if you're willing to invest the time to learn how to do it well, you can master it.

The Effects of Boiling Temperature

Increasing your boiling time won't really give you the desired effect unless you have the right temperature. Weak, wimpy heating of the wort won't do much for your beer. Among other things, the physical action of a rolling boil helps to drive off the unwanted molecules and increases the hot break by literally bringing proteins and phenols into contact with each other. The addition of Irish Moss (also called *copper finings*), a polymer of starch that proteins stick easily to, also improves the efficiency of the hot break. To make sure your wort boils at the proper temperature for the right amount of time, don't start timing the process until you see active and significant signs of boiling. In summary, when you boil, make sure you're *really* boiling. Your beer will be much better for it.

On the other hand, don't overdo it. Every brewer has probably experienced a boilover in their time, which not only wastes beer but also makes a very gooey, sticky mess. This problem can be easily solved by leaving the lid of the boiling pot slightly ajar, allowing steam to escape. As discussed on page 54, how much you crack the lid will also affect how well other flavors and aromas are extracted and kept in your beer.

How to Add Specialty Grains and Fruit

For the extract brewer, the wort boil is also the time when special grains (and their associated tastes and characteristics) can be added to the beer. However, boiling these grains easily extracts tannins and husk oils, leading to astringency and huskiness in the wort. Therefore, specialty grains should only be added to cold or room-temperature water, before heat is applied. When the wort does boil, remove the grains within 5 minutes of achieving a rolling boil. This is extremely easy to do if the grains are in small, permeable bags (similar to nylon socks), usually available from your favorite homebrew supply headquarters. When the time comes to remove the bags, pick them out with tongs and squeeze between two dinner plates to release all the good malt juice. You can even use the spent grains to fertilize your favorite plants — but make sure you bury them; bacteria in the air love spent grains, too, and you may end up with a rotting mass instead of plant food.

Many fruit skins contain the same tannins as grain husks, so a boiled fruit skin will result in the same astringent flavors (think of the tart, sometimes puckering flavor of a red wine, which comes from grape skins). The best way to get fruit flavors and aromas without the astringency is to add fruit to your fermenter. Sanitize the fruit by placing it in water that's just under boiling temperature for 15 to 30 minutes and then add it to the fermenter. For optimal aroma, add the fruit after the first few days of fermentation (so the vigorous bubbling doesn't drive off the fruit smells). If you insist on boiling your fruit in the wort, minimize the boiling time. You can also try adding the fruit to the warm, but not boiling, wort while it's cooling. Store-bought concentrates can be used, although the result is usually lower quality than with real fruit.

Adding Hops (Bittering/Flavoring/Aromatic)

Perhaps the most interactive process during the actual boiling of the wort is the addition of hops, which contributes the desired bitterness level and the hops flavors and aromas. Hops are much like tea leaves; each hop type has a specific flavor. When the hops are in contact with boiling water, oils and other molecules are drawn out of the hop glands. However, some of these molecules can quickly evaporate out of the wort. Hops are added at distinct phases of the wort boil depending on the types of flavors and aromas desired. These phases include bittering hops, flavoring hops, and aromatic hops (we won't consider **dry hopping**, since it takes place in the fermenter, not the boiling pot). **Bittering hops**, added to the boiling wort for 30 to 60 minutes, gives the bitter hop bite, which defines many styles of beer. **Flavoring hops**, added to the boiling wort for 10 to 15 minutes, gives special spicy, floral, fruity, or other desired hops flavors. One to 2 minutes of **aromatic hops** in the boiling wort can add classic aromas to your beer.

The type and amount of hops, and the time they are added to the boiling wort, are determined by the individual brewer as the **hops schedule**, simply a plan of which hops you choose and how long you boil them. These choices, to a good extent, define an important part of your beer. An excellent review of the specific flavors from each hop species and their standard uses (boiling/flavoring/aromatic) is given in Papazian's *New Complete Joy of Homebrewing* (see page 109).

Choosing the Best Wort Volume

For extract and extract/specialty-grain brewers, the amount of water used to start the wort boil can make a big difference in the amount of grain and hops goodies that end up in your beer. The volume matters because it affects how the molecules dissolve in the boiling wort. During the wort boil, all these molecules are being drawn out (*extracted*) from the grain or hop leaf, some are chemically rearranging (*isomerizing*), and all are trying to dissolve in the water. The problem is that if the concentration of sugars, proteins, oils, and other flavoring molecules is very high, the water may not be able to extract and dissolve all the molecules. You can overcome this problem by providing enough water to dissolve as many of the molecules out as possible. Just think about trying to make table sugar dissolve in water — a little goes in fine, but a lot just won't dissolve no matter how hard you try. (Then think about how much easier it is to dissolve sugar in hot water versus cold; that's one reason why a good, strong wort boil will help in extraction of grains and hops.)

However (yes, there's always a "however"), you probably don't want to start with 5 gallons (18.9 liters) of water to boil your wort because it's hard to work with, it will probably boil over in a standard boiling pot, and it's a lot harder to cool quickly when using standard wort cooling tricks. A workable solution is start the wort boil with about 2 gallons (7.6 liters) of water for lighter beers and about 3 gallons (11.4 liters) for darker beers. These amounts accomplish proper extraction of grains and hops, but still allow 2 to 3 gallons (7.6 to 11.4 liters) of space for controlled boils and quick cooling.

One of the fastest ways to cool wort is to just pour 3 gallons (11.4 liters) of ice cold water into 2 gallons (7.6 liters) of boiled wort. This technique can produce cooling times as fast as 15 to 30 seconds. For larger volumes, an ice bath in your sink or bathtub, and/or frozen 2-liter soda bottles of water (sanitized just before use) immersed in the wort will give you fast, efficient wort cooling. For the high-tech brewer, standard immersion wort coolers are also very useful.

The Advantages of Cracking the Lid

As noted earlier, cracking the lid on your boiling pot helps eliminate dreaded wort boilovers. The degree to which you do this can also influence good and bad tastes that end up in your final brew. A lot of molecules from the specialty grains, extract, or hops need to evaporate out of the wort so that an off flavor won't result. A closed or barely cracked lid will trap these molecules, directing them right back into the beer. Molecules you want to get out include diacetyl, dimethyl sulfide (DMS), and harsh hop oils. So, crack your lid a few inches during the wort boil to release these undesired molecules. It's also not a bad idea to remove the lid completely a few times to let the condensation escape; a lot of what's in that condensation needs to get out. You'll probably be doing this anyway to add hops, Irish Moss, and any specialty adjuncts during the boil period.

You'll want to keep other things in your pot, though, mainly the very volatile hop acids that will give your beer nice hops aromas and flavors. You also don't want all of your nice wort to evaporate into thin air, so don't leave the lid completely off; otherwise what's left of your beer may not have any flavor at all. During the addition of aromatic hops (the last 1 or 2 minutes of the boil), leave the lid completely on (unless you're in danger of boiling over); by that time everything that needs to get out is out, and you want to keep in all those great hop aromas.

Summary of Successful Mashing, Sparging, and Boiling

PROCESS	DESIRED RESULT	TIPS FOR SUCCESS
Mash-in	Mix grains with hot water.	Use proper temperature.
Acid Rest	Allow pH to drop.	Used only for selected malts.
Protein Rest	Allow proteins to break down.	Usually only for selected styles.
Starch Conversion	Allow large sugars to break down.	Major step in mashing important for all styles.
Mash-out	Kill mash enzymes by high temperatures.	Don't go above 168°F (75.6°C).
Sparging	Obtain sugars and proteins for wort.	Watch temperature and pH of water.
Wort Boil	Sanitize, clarify, beer character, hops addition, volume reduction.	Keep at a rolling boil for at least 30 to 60 minutes.

5. Understanding and Avoiding Off Flavors

Almost every step of homebrewing, from developing a recipe to bottling or kegging, can create some kind of off flavor. Unfortunately, even one off flavor can ruin an entire batch of beer. Despite this fact, one of the aspects of homebrewing least appreciated by homebrewers is an understanding of these off flavors, particularly where they come from and how they can be avoided in the future. Beginning brewing books often contain directions on how to avoid off flavors, but with no explanation why. The result is these critical actions are often glossed over and forgotten by the homebrewer. This chapter includes a thorough explanation of the causes of standard off flavors that often plague the unwary homebrewer and directions on how to avoid them.

ACETYLALDEHYDE

Off Flavor

Freshly cut, green apples and/or acetic-cider/rotten-apple smell and flavor.

Source

Acetylaldehyde is one of the chemicals along the normal chain of fermentation (see illustration, page 40). Normally acetylaldehyde will be processed to ethanol. However, in young beer or beer with a high alcohol content, this final conversion may not be completed — an effect especially evident when weak yeast is used — resulting in the smell and flavor of freshly cut, little green apples. Additionally, ethanol can be reversibly oxidized (see page 75) back to acetylaldehyde and acetic acid. The combination of the apple smell and the acetic acid give an "acetic-cider"/rotten-apple smell and taste. A third source of acetylaldehyde off flavor is bacterial infection, which creates a rotten-apple taste probably due to other bacteria-derived flavors.

To Avoid

Use good-quality yeast, especially when brewing high-alcohol beer styles. Allow beer to ferment and age for the proper amount of time. Eliminate bacterial infections by maintaining sterile brewing techniques.

ALCOHOLIC/SOLVENTLIKE

Off Flavor

Disagreeable alcohol flavor. Banana, rose, bitter, chemical (acetone or lacquer thinner), hot, or spicy flavors. Undesirable warming, prickly effect in the mouth and throat.

Source

The sweet flavor of ethanol, a two-carbon form of alcohol, is obviously desired in beer. Longer chain alcohols, including propanol (three carbons), butanol (four carbons), and related molecules are desired in limited quantities in high-alcohol beers like strong ales and barley wines or in certain beer styles such as bocks/double bocks. However, excessive amounts of these larger alcohol molecules, the so-called fusel alcohols

---

MOLECULES CONTRIBUTING TO ALCOHOLIC SOLVENTLIKE OFF FLAVORS

$CH_3CH_2CH_2OH$

Propanol
(disagreeable alcohol taste)

$CH_3CH_2CH_2CH_2OH$

Butanol
(disagreeable alcohol taste)

CH_3
|
$CH_3CHCH_2CH_2OH$

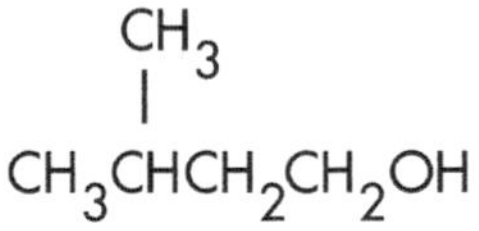

Isobutanol
(disagreeable alcohol taste)

CH_3
|
$CH_3CH_2CHCH_2OH$

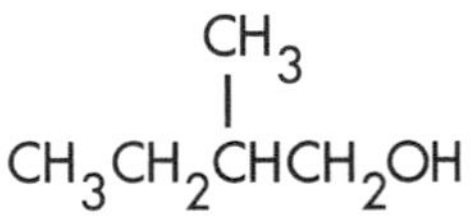

Isoamyl Alcohol
(banana, solventlike taste)

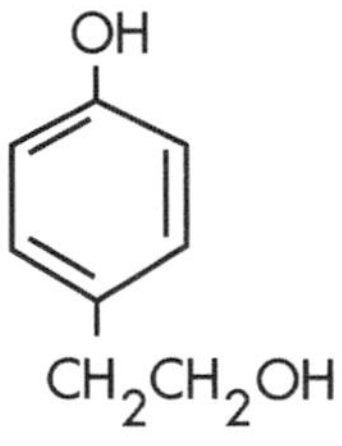

OH

CH_2CH_2OH

Tyrosol
(roses, bitter, chemical taste)

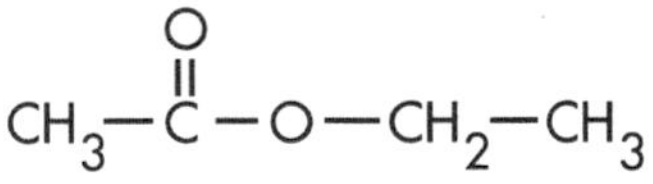

$$CH_3-\overset{\overset{O}{\|}}{C}-O-CH_2-CH_3$$

Ethyl Acetate
(fruity, solventlike taste)

The presence of any of these molecules in beer can result in alcoholic/solventlike off flavors and undesirable tastes, as noted.

(propanol, butanol, isobutanol, isoamyl alcohol) and phenolic alcohols (tyrosol), create a number of disagreeable off flavors, especially in lighter beer styles. Ethyl acetate, formed by the combination of ethanol and acetic acid, is often a major contributor to a solventlike off flavor.

These undesirable alcohol/solventlike tastes can be due to a number of causes, including high fermentation temperatures, excessive yeast growth, excessive levels of amino acids and their resulting metabolism, and/or high levels of ethanol that don't allow normal fermentation. Oxidation can also cause ethanol to be converted to some of these higher alcohols.

In summary, fermentation that's too fast or too strong or uses the wrong starting material (say, amino acids instead of sugars) can overload the normal ethanol-producing pathway, resulting in undesired products. Too much ethanol will also result in these alternative fermentation pathways if the yeast are weak or if the beer is too old. Bacterial infections also lead to alcoholic and solventlike molecules (especially ethyl acetate).

To Avoid

Choose yeast strains appropriate for style so high amounts of ethanol won't overwhelm a weaker yeast strain and produce improper levels of higher alcohols. Be careful with especially strong yeast strains isolated for high-alcohol beers. Control excessive amino acid content by proper recipe formulation. Control fermentation temperatures. Maintain sterile brewing conditions.

ASTRINGENT

Off Flavor

Drying, puckering taste felt throughout the mouth. Can be

tannin, vinegary, or tart sensation. Can also feel like metallic or powdery coating of mouth.

Source

Major sources of astringency include boiled grain husks, fruit skins, excessive hopping, or wort trub. Astringency results from polyphenols, also called *tannins* because they were and are often used to tan animal hides. This off flavor is more noticeable in lighter, drier beers than in stronger, sweeter beers.

Tannins (see illustration), are usually found in the outer layers of the grain kernel, particularly the husk. Their extraction from grain husks results from overzealous crushing

MOLECULES CONTRIBUTING TO ASTRINGENT OFF FLAVORS

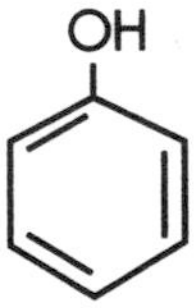

Phenol

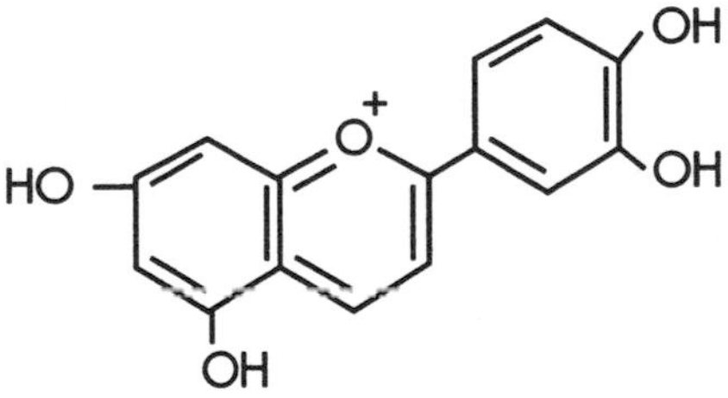

Cyanidin (Anthocyanogen)

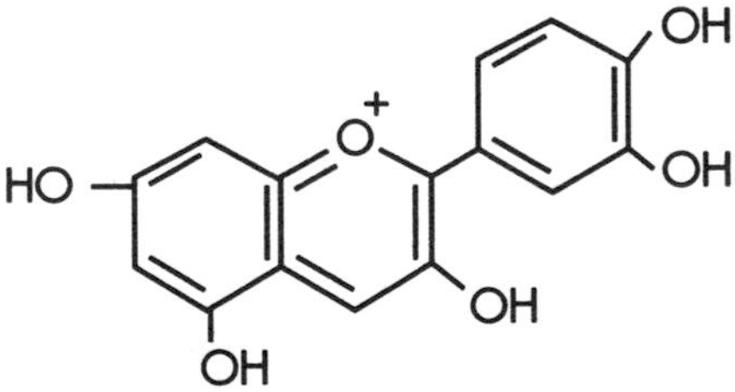

Flavin-3-ol- (+) -Catachin

Phenol and polyphenolic molecules (tannins) contribute to astringency, a dry, puckering taste reminiscent of dry red wines.

of the grain kernels, overly alkaline mashes or sparge water, or excessive amounts of sparge water. Similarly, boiling specialty grains will release tannins into the wort. These grains should only be in the boiling pot up to the start of a boil.

Like grain husks, fruit skins also contain tannins. The dry, puckering feeling produced by red wines is, in fact, tannins from grape skins, although in that case the taste is desired. When real fruit is used for beer making, the homebrewer should never boil it in the wort. Instead, sanitize the fruit by placing it in water that is just below boiling temperature for 15 to 30 minutes. After it has been sanitized, fruit can be added to the fermenter, preferably after the first few days of fermentation (so the vigorous bubbling doesn't drive off your fruit smells).

Over-hopping can lead to astringency when excess hop oils and resins are converted to polyphenolic-anthocyanogens (see illustration on page 61). Astringency can also result from poor separation of the *krausen* and the fermenting wort. More exactly, the brown layer of scum that builds up on top of fermenting beer during the initial stages of fermentation is filled with tannins from hops and husks. If this layer is not removed from the wort by a *blow-off tube*, the wort will reabsorb the tannin off flavors. Finally, bacterial contamination can also cause astringency, although the bacteria usually produce an acetic acid or vinegary off flavor as well.

To Avoid

Proper crushing of grains is essential to avoid astringency. The grain should be lightly cracked but never torn, shredded, or crushed. If you are mashing and sparging, pay careful attention to the temperature and alkalinity of the mash and sparge water as well as to the amount of sparge water used. In this case, more is definitely not better. If using specialty grains, heat the water to boiling and then remove the grain bags. If using whole fruits, never boil the fruits in the wort, and keep the time that the wort is exposed to the skins to a minimum. Over-hopping of beer must be avoided unless extra steps are taken to separate the offending tannins. One easy step is the use of a blow-off tube during the first two to three days of fermenta-tion. Finally, avoid bacterial contamination.

CHLOROPHENOLS

Off Flavor

Plasticlike taste.

Source

Chlorophenols and the associated plastic taste result from the use of chlorinated water or mistakenly added chlorine. The molecular chlorine in the water combines with phenols found in the wort, creating the chlorophenols. The three types of chlorophenols that can be created are illustrated below.

MOLECULES CONTRIBUTING TO CHLOROPHENOL OFF FLAVORS

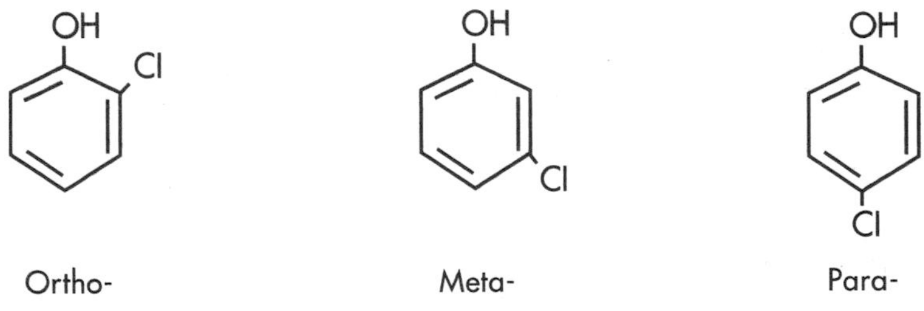

Ortho-   Meta-   Para-

The three types of chlorophenols (ortho-, meta-, and para-). The position of the chloride on the benzene ring determines the exact type of chlorophenol as well as its chemical qualities.

To Avoid

Don't use chlorinated water. If you have chlorinated water and need to use it for brewing, use a filter that removes chlorine or boil the water for approximately 15 minutes to drive off the chlorine, then cool to room temperature.

DIACETYL

Off Flavor

Butter or butterscotch. "Slickness" on the tongue.

Source

Diacetyl is produced by all yeast as a natural part of fermentation but then is subsequently processed during a normal fermentation cycle to neutrally flavored molecules. This process occurs in two major steps known as *production* and *reduction*. If any of these steps are blocked or slowed, high levels of diacetyl may result.

PATHWAY OF PRODUCTION OF DIACETYL

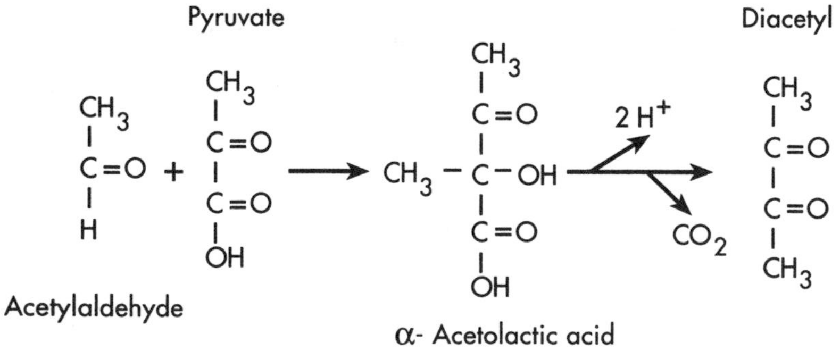

This normal process in yeast fermentation is usually followed by reduction of the diacetyl.

Production

Production of diacetyl involves the combination of acetylaldehyde and pyruvate (see illustration on previous page) to form α-acetolactic acid, which then forms diacetyl.

Reduction

Reduction of diacetyl includes a chemical change to acetoin, which gives an unpleasant fruity or musty flavor, and then to 2,3-butanediol (as illustrated on page 66), which imparts no flavor or smell to the beer.

Another minor relative of diacetyl is 2,3-pentanedione which imparts a honeylike flavor to beer. This molecule is rarely formed and so is considered unimportant.

Several factors can increase diacetyl by slowing its reduction to 2,3-butanediol. These include:

* Worts with high amounts of sugars and starches
* Worts low in the amino acid *valine* which promotes proper reduction of diacetyl
* Decreased flocculation and settling of yeast by weak yeast strains and/or premature wort cooling
* Defective yeast produced by spontaneous mutations that have lost their ability to reduce diacetyl
* Abbreviated wort boiling — increased temperature initially increases diacetyl production but then promotes its reduction (short boils won't allow completion of the second, diacetyl-reduction stage)
* Excess oxygen in the wort, which causes diacetyl production by alternative reaction pathways

Alternately, diactyl levels will *decrease* if any of the following actions are taken:

* Strong boils of at least one-hour duration
* Good wort recipes that provide yeast cells with all essential nutrients
* Healthy, strong yeast cells with good flocculation and sedimenting characteristics
* Warmer fermentation temperatures, probably by increasing yeast metabolism, including diacetyl reduction (although this method may only be realistically possible for ales)

Excessive diacetyl can also result from a bacterial contamination (sometimes called *sarcina sickness*, after the offending bacterial strain). These bacteria tend to grow most rapidly during the end of wort fermentation and stay closely and almost irreversibly associated with the yeast. Therefore, if a batch of wort is contaminated with diacetyl-producing bacteria, any batches of wort using repitching of that yeast will also be infected.

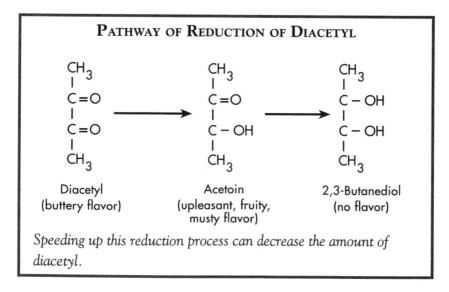

PATHWAY OF REDUCTION OF DIACETYL

Diacetyl
(buttery flavor)

Acetoin
(upleasant, fruity, musty flavor)

2,3-Butanediol
(no flavor)

Speeding up this reduction process can decrease the amount of diacetyl.

To Avoid

Boil wort at a rolling boil for at least 1 hour. Formulate recipes to give yeast all the necessary nutrients. Use good-quality, healthy yeast. Allow yeast to start initial growth before pitching. Avoid excessive oxygenation of wort, especially after yeast pitching. Allow time for full fermentation. Maintain sterile brewing conditions.

DIMETHYL SULFIDE (DMS)

Off Flavor

Sweet, cooked corn, celery, parsnip, shellfish, or oysterlike aromas and flavors.

Source

DMS is produced by cleavage of S-methyl methionine (SMM), a derivative of the amino acid methionine, which is a product of malt germination. Bacterial infections also produce DMS by converting dimethyl sulfoxide (DMSO) into DMS.

PATHWAY OF PRODUCTION OF DIMETHYL SULFIDE (DMS)

	Dimethyl sulfide (DMS)	Dimethyl sulfoxide (DMSO)
S-Methylmethionine (SMM)		

$$CH_3 \quad \quad \quad \quad H \quad O \atop S-CH_2-CH_2-C-C-OH \atop CH_3 \quad \quad \quad \quad NH_2 \quad \xrightarrow{\textit{Natural}} \quad CH_3 \atop S \atop CH_3 \quad \xleftarrow{\textit{Bacterial}} \quad CH_3 \atop S=O \atop CH_3$$

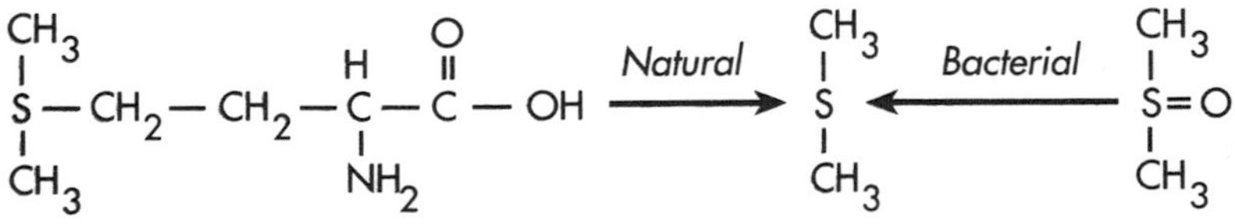

DMS can be produced either by natural processes in malt germination or by bacterial infection.

To Avoid

Levels of DMS from malt germination can be controlled by limiting the amount of SMM produced by proper germination length and temperature. Unless the homebrewer is also germinating his or her own malt, this is largely out of their control. However, any good malt supplier will understand the problem with improper germination conditions and make sure to avoid them. If you continually encounter bad SMM and resulting DMS problems and the only explanation appears to be the grain source, choose a different supplier.

The normal amounts of SMM and, therefore, DMS found in grains is properly removed by simple evaporation during wort boiling. In fact, the amount of DMS is directly proportional to the amount of time spent above 158°F (70°C) during the wort boil. Short or weak boils won't let DMS evaporate, leaving it in the beer. Slow cooling of the wort is also responsible for excess DMS levels. Therefore, worts should be allowed to remain at full boil for a minimum of 1 hour and quickly and efficiently cooled to pitching temperatures. Additionally, DMS is removed by gaseous CO_2 "scrubbing" during fermentation: In essence, the rising CO_2 bubbles help carry away remaining DMS. If fermentation is weak, this scrubbing effect will be decreased. Finally, a clean, sterile technique eliminates any bacterial infections that may cause DMS production from DMSO.

FRUITY/ESTERY

Off Flavor

Inappropriate aroma and flavor of sweet fruits, including banana, grapefruit, raspberry, pear, apple, or strawberry.

Source

Esters are naturally produced by the combination of alcohols and acids found in the wort. Certain yeast strains produce specific esters, yielding characteristic fruit flavors and aromas that are proper in certain styles of beer, especially ales.

PRODUCTION OF AN ESTER FROM AN ALCOHOL AND ACID

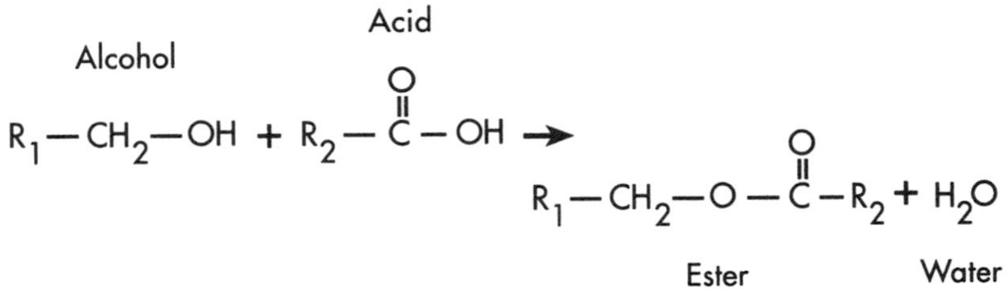

$$R_1-CH_2-OH + R_2-\overset{\overset{O}{\|}}{C}-OH \rightarrow$$

$$R_1-CH_2-O-\overset{\overset{O}{\|}}{C}-R_2 + H_2O$$

Alcohol   Acid   Ester   Water

Some ester flavors are acceptable in certain beer styles, especially many ales. R_1 and R_2 in the figures refer to any carbon chains of any length. The specific nature of these chains, generally, do not affect this reaction.

COMMON ESTERS AND THEIR ASSOCIATED FLAVORS

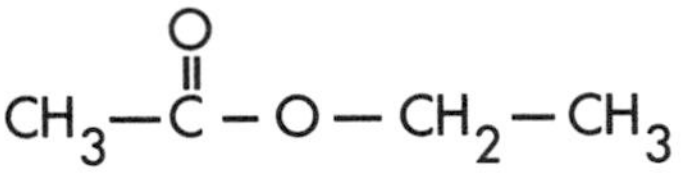

$$CH_3-\overset{\overset{O}{\|}}{C}-O-CH_2-CH_3$$

Ethyl Acetate
(fruity/solventlike flavor)

Isoamyl Acetate
(banana flavor)

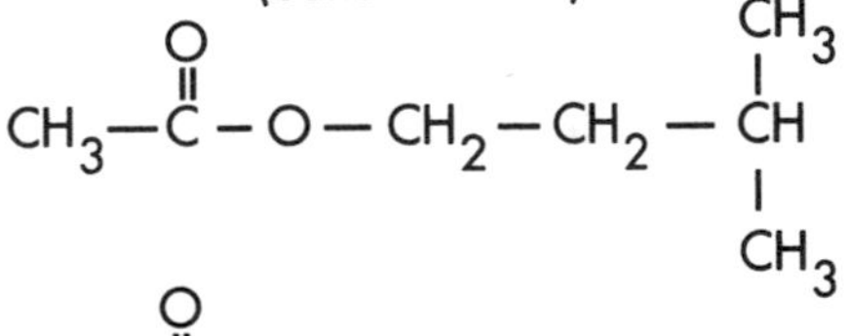

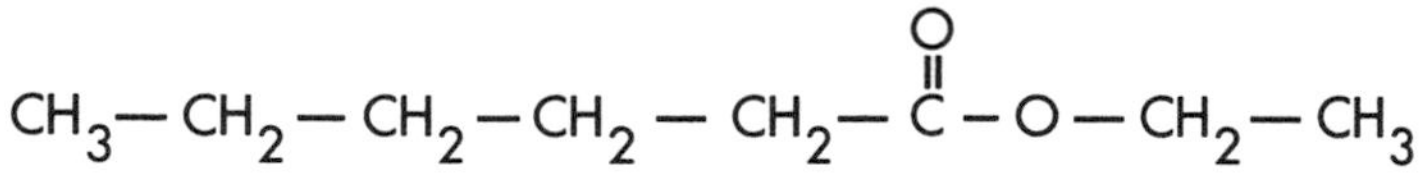

$$CH_3-\overset{\overset{O}{\|}}{C}-O-CH_2-CH_2-\overset{\overset{CH_3}{|}}{CH}{\underset{|}{_{CH_3}}}$$

$$CH_3-CH_2-CH_2-CH_2-CH_2-\overset{\overset{O}{\|}}{C}-O-CH_2-CH_3$$

Ethyl Hexanoate (apple flavor)

Ester flavors are usually described as very sweet and fruity tastes and aromas.

Effect of Temperature on Ester Formation
(Ales and Lagers)

BEER CATEGORY	TEMPERATURE (DEGREES FAHRENHEIT)	ESTER CONTENT
ALE	60 to 65	Low
	65 to 75	Medium
	> 75	High
LAGER	< 50	Low
	50 to 55	Medium
	> 55	High

The creation of esters and normal yeast respiration are competing processes, so low oxygen levels or high yeast pitching rates in the initial wort (which decreases yeast respiration) will lead to increased ester production. High starting gravities and fermentation temperatures will also yield excess ester flavors, including those illustrated at the bottom of the previous page.

To Avoid

Maintain proper fermentation temperature (see table above). Use proper yeast for the right beer category (ale/lager) and style. Do not overpitch yeast. Properly oxygenate wort before initial yeast pitching.

GRASSY

Off Flavor

Musty smell characteristic of freshly cut grass, sometimes resulting from activity of bacteria that metabolize **barley**.

Source

Production of cis-3-Hexanal by bacterial metabolism of barley. This rare effect is not commonly encountered by home-brewers. See George Fix's article, "A Homebrewer's Guide to Beer Flavor Descriptors" in *Zymurgy* for more information (see reading list page 109).

To Avoid

Store malt in cool, dry area and avoid crushing malts until just before use to eliminate unwanted bacterial metabolism.

HAZE (CHILL OR PERMANENT)

Off Flavor

Cloudiness due to precipitation of medium and/or high molecular weight proteins or protein-tannin complexes, ß-glycan or pentosan sugars, or metal ions.

Source

Chill and permanent haze are indications of poor malting, mashing and/or boiling techniques that haven't properly broken down wort proteins or sugars. Unusual additions or levels of ions (calcium, copper, iron, lead, tin, or silicate) may also cause haze. Chill haze is usually seen upon chilling of beer, which causes the aggregation and precipitation of proteins. Chill haze is reversible upon warming since usually the medium–molecular weight proteins involved redissolve easily. Permanent haze, as its name indicates, is not reversible and is associated with high–molecular weight proteins or sugars that won't redissolve. Haze may also result from poor and/or slow wort cooling, which decreases the break.

To Avoid

Use properly malted grains. Break down large proteins and sugars in the wort by following proper mashing conditions and times carefully and boiling wort for a full hour at a rolling boil. Use fining agents, such as Irish Moss, if necessary. Quickly and efficiently cool the wort after the boil by adding cold water; immersing the boil pot in an ice bath; or submerging sterile, frozen, 2-liter bottles (see Chapter 4).

Hoppy

Off Flavor

Overabundance of noble-type hop flavor for beer style.

Source

Although not technically an off flavor, too much hops for a certain style of beer is as incorrect as any other problem. Excess hop aroma comes from a high amount of the hop oil humulene, found in abundance in the so-called noble hops.

To Avoid

Formulate your recipe for the beer style being brewed, including hop amounts, types, and hop schedule.

HUMULENE MOLECULE

Humulene, a hop constituent gives so-called elegant and refined aromas and flavors. Humulene is found in high amounts in noble hops varieties and is considered incorrect in certain beer styles.

HUSKY/GRAINY

Off Flavor

Dry, bitter, cardboardy, or harsh taste of raw grain husks sometimes encountered by all-grain brewers. Huskiness is not to be confused with tannins/astringency or oxidation off flavors. However, tannins can result directly from husk flavors through oxidation.

Source

Torn, shredded, or over-crushed grains giving wort the taste of the grain husk. Burned mash or overly alkaline mash and sparging water.

To Avoid

Crush malt gently, breaking but not tearing, shredding, or crushing the grain. If mashing, maintain proper mash and sparge acidity.

LIGHT-STRUCK/SKUNKY

Off Flavor

Mild or strong aroma of a skunk. Found in beer exposed to light, usually due to bottling in clear or green bottles.

Source

Light-struck off flavor, more commonly called *skunky*, is caused by a breakdown of the hop alpha-acid humulone followed by a reaction with hydrogen sulfide, creating the molecule 3-methyl-2-butene-1-thiol, commonly known as a mercaptan. This mercaptan is the same molecule that skunks emit to create their infamous aroma. This process is caused by blue-green light (400 to 520 nanometer wavelength), which is absorbed by brown bottles but passes unchanged through clear or green bottles.

FORMATION OF "SKUNKY" MERCAPTAN FROM HUMULONE ALPHA-ACID

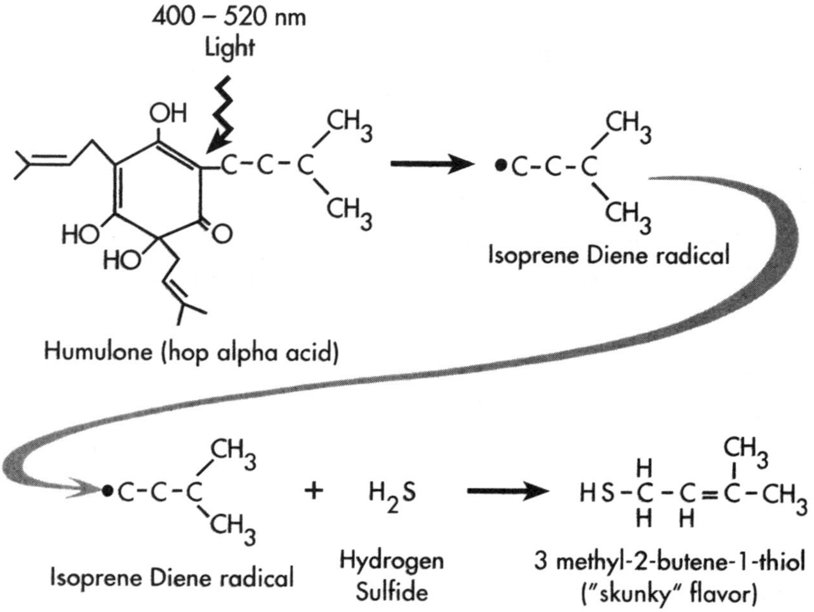

400 – 520 nm
Light

Humulone (hop alpha acid)

Isoprene Diene radical

•C–C–C + H_2S ⟶ $HS–C–C=C–CH_3$

Isoprene Diene radical

Hydrogen
Sulfide

3 methyl-2-butene-1-thiol
("skunky" flavor)

These sulfur-containing mercaptan molecules result from the inappropriate exposure of beer to unfiltered light, leading to the alternative name "light-struck." The symbol • denotes a highly reactive carbon atom, which has been "energized" by the light ray.

To Avoid

Use only brown bottles; they may not look as cool as clear or green bottles, but a skunk in your beer is even less cool. Also, protect your clear-glass fermenter from sunlight or strong room light. A simple brown paper bag cover with a hole cut for the bubbler will work well.

METALLIC

Off Flavor

Taste of metals, especially iron, that can also be felt on the tip of the tongue, the front upper arch of the mouth, and the rear of the throat. Also described as tinny, coinlike, or bloodlike.

Source

Contact of wort or beer with uncoated or unprocessed metallic surfaces, especially iron-containing surfaces. Examples include metal (but not stainless steel) boiling pots, metal fittings, iron-containing water and grains, iron-containing filters, and uncoated metal bottle caps and kegs.

To Avoid

Keep wort and beer away from anything containing uncoated metal parts, especially iron-containing materials. Use iron-free water, grains, and filters.

OXIDATION

Off Flavor

Winey, wet cardboard, papery, rotten or old vegetables, pineapple, sherry, baby diapers, or nutty. Increasing sourness, harshness, and bitterness.

Source

Oxidation can take place among a number of the components of beer, especially during aging and storage, to give a variety of what is described as stale and old flavors. Oxidation involves the interaction of oxygen and the molecules in beer, a process increased by high temperatures. Oxygen can get into the wort and beer in a variety of ways, but the most common include continued aeration of the fermenting wort after the yeast pitching and unnecessary aeration or excessive head space in kegs or bottles.

Off Flavors Produced by the Oxidation of Various Components

BEER COMPONENT	OFF FLAVOR(S) PRODUCED BY OXIDATION
Alcohols	
Ethanol Products	
Acetic Acid	Vinegar
Melanoidin Products	
Oxidized alcohols and aldehydes (from malting and wort)	Winey, sherry, rotten vegetables and fruits, baby diapers
Humulones (Hops α-acids)	Stale, "cheesy"
Hop Oils	
Humulene Products	
Humulenol	Sagebrushlike
Humulene Epoxide	Haylike, moldy
Humelol	Haylike
Myrcene Products	
Linalool/Geraniol	Floral, herbal
Lipids/Fatty Acids	Soapy, fatty, goaty, sweaty Can interact with alcohols to produce fruity esters.
Proteins/Amino Acids	Aldehydes (Little green apple smell and flavor)
Phenols (Tannins)	Harsh, bitter, and astringent

To Avoid

In a world filled with oxygen, oxidation can never be eliminated, but it can be reduced to almost undetectable levels. Steps to reduce oxidation include keeping any extra oxygen out of the beer beyond what is necessary for initial yeast *aerobic,* or "with oxygen," respiration. Therefore, only aerate your beer when initially transferring the fresh wort to the fermenter for pitching of the yeast. After that point, minimize any shaking or mixing of the wort, especially when racking the beer to a secondary fermenter or removing it from the trub before bottling or kegging. Also, leave only about ½ to 1 inch (1.27 cm to 2.54 cm) of head space during bottling and age and store beer in a relatively cool environment. Special bottling caps that absorb any remaining oxygen may also limit oxidation. These caps are available from most homebrew supply shops.

Remember that oxidation of hops is sometimes desired (for example, Cascade hops), but usually these compounds give undesired flavors or aromas. To avoid this problem, store hops in the freezer in sealed plastic bags and don't use them if the glands are orange. That means they're old and oxidized.

PHENOLIC/MEDICINAL

Off Flavor

Medicinal, plastic, electrical fire, antiseptic mouthwash, adhesive strip bandage, smoky, or clovelike off flavor and especially aroma.

Source

A variety of phenolic compounds are found in beer. Many are desired flavors and smells, especially hop acids and clovelike phenols that are proper in wheat-style beers. However, a larger group of phenolic compounds impart disagreeable flavors to beer and have to be controlled through good brewing practices. These include the solventlike phenols (see "Alcoholic/Solventlike"), the tannins (see "Astringency"), and the chlorophenols. Other phenols impart what's best described as a medicinal aroma and flavor to the beer. These unwanted phenolic compounds are almost always extracted during mashing and sparging due to improper temperature, pH, and amounts of sparge water. Certain wild yeast strains, which produce high amounts of phenols, can also infect worts.

To Avoid

Use proper sparging techniques, especially temperature, pH, and amount of sparge water. Establish and maintain sterile brewing techniques to avoid contamination by wild yeast. Discard plastic fermentation vessels if cuts or scratches are evident.

PHENOLIC MOLECULES

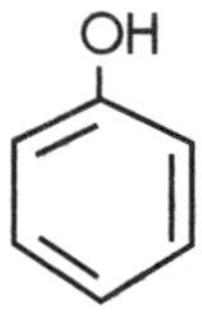

Phenol

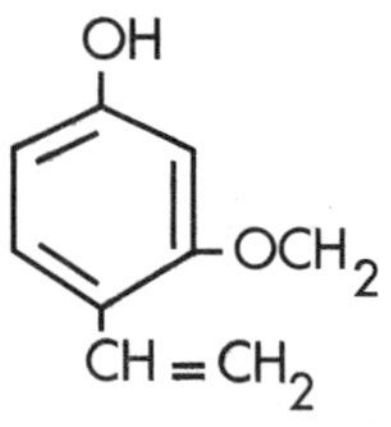

4-Vinyl Guaiacol
(clovelike flavor)

Molecules containing several phenol rings give medicinal off flavors. The phenolic compound 4-vinyl guaiacol, proper in wheat beers, gives clovelike flavors and aromas.

SALTY

Off Flavor

Taste of table salt (sodium chloride) or any of the other flavors from ions (see table on page 15). Saltiness is detected on the front sides of the tongue.

Source

The addition of salts adds certain flavor characteristics or increases solubility and taste contributions of grains and hops. Certain beer styles (say, Burton Ales) are known for the intricate and subtle combination of ion flavors from dissolved salts. However, too much of a good thing can be bad . . . very bad. For example, excess table salt (sodium chloride) will produce salty beer — certainly a very undesirable taste. Excess Epsom salts (magnesium sulfate) will break down to magnesium chloride, giving beer a very bitter flavor. Too much gypsum (calcium sulfate) will give beer an overly dry, sharp flavor.

To Avoid

Don't add salt to your brewing water without first knowing: a) the ion content of the water, b) the proper amount of each ion required in the style of beer being brewed, and c) how much salt to add to achieve the desired taste or solubility effect.

SOUR/ACIDIC

Off Flavor

Pungent, sharp, or tart taste in beer, including vinegar, rubber, sour milk, or acidic/salty flavors. Sour/acidic off flavors are noted on the sides of the tongue or, in cases of high contamination levels, throughout the mouth and throat.

COMMON MOLECULES RESPONSIBLE FOR SOUR/ACIDIC OFF FLAVORS

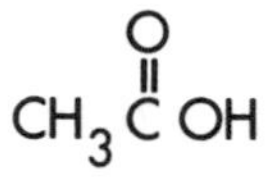

$$CH_3 \overset{\overset{\textstyle O}{\|}}{C} OH$$

Acetic Acid
(vinegar taste)

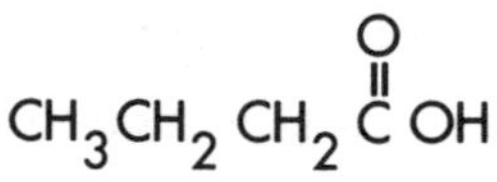

$$CH_3 CH_2 CH_2 \overset{\overset{\textstyle O}{\|}}{C} OH$$

Butyric Acid
(rubber taste)

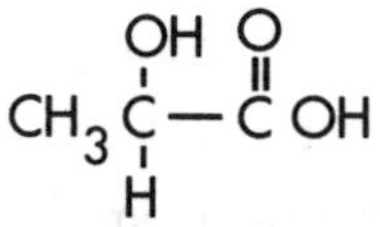

$$CH_3 \overset{\overset{\textstyle OH}{|}}{\underset{\underset{\textstyle H}{|}}{C}} - \overset{\overset{\textstyle O}{\|}}{C} OH$$

Lactic Acid
(sour taste)

$$CH_3 \overset{\overset{\textstyle O}{\|}}{C} - \overset{\overset{\textstyle O}{\|}}{C} OH$$

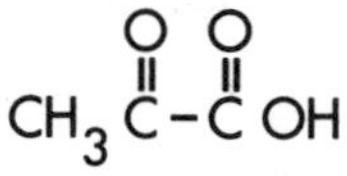

Pyruvic Acid
(salty taste)

These sour/acidic flavors are easily noted on the back sides of the tongue. They usually only result from bacterial infections.

Source

Bacterial infection and the resulting production of small organic acids (see illustration above).

To Avoid

Establish and maintain sanitary and sterile brewing conditions.

SULFURLIKE/ROTTEN EGG/BURNING MATCH

Off Flavor

Smell and taste of rotten eggs or a burning match (hydrogen sulfide).

Source

Small amounts of hydrogen sulfide are a natural product of yeast fermentation (in particular, metabolism of the amino acids methionine and cysteine). However, the small amount of hydrogen sulfide produced by this process won't normally be

THE AMINO ACIDS METHIONINE AND CYSTEINE

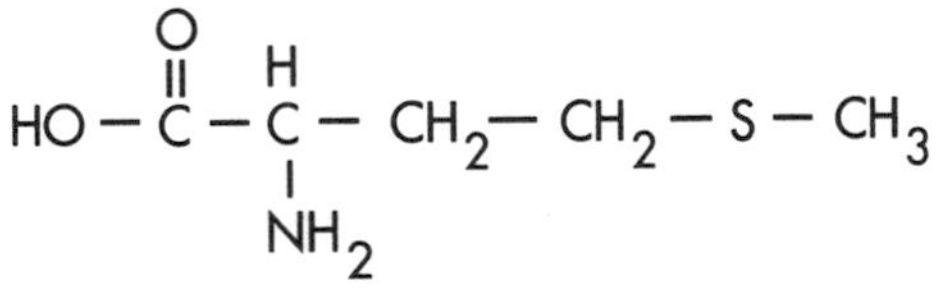

$$HO - \overset{\overset{O}{\|}}{C} - \overset{\overset{H}{|}}{\underset{\underset{NH_2}{|}}{C}} - CH_2 - CH_2 - S - CH_3$$

Methionine

$$HO - \overset{\overset{O}{\|}}{C} - \overset{\overset{H}{|}}{\underset{\underset{NH_2}{|}}{C}} - CH_2 - SH$$

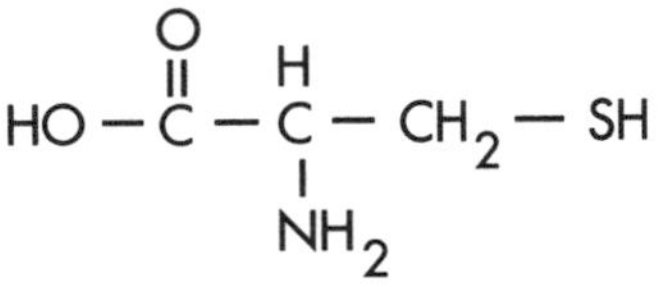

Cysteine

Normal yeast fermentation converts the sulfur (S) in these molecules to hydrogen sulfide (H$_2$S). Excessive amounts of either methionine or cysteine and, therefore, hydrogen sulfide will result in the off flavor sulfurlike/rotten egg/burning match.

noticed in beer. Additionally, a large amount of this hydrogen sulfide is removed during fermentation by the "scrubbing" effect of rising CO$_2$ bubbles.

Excess hydrogen sulfide that would cause a noticeable off flavor is almost always caused by a bacterial infection. Increased fermentation temperature can increase this off flavor. Larger sulfur-containing molecules can also produce powerful off flavors, most giving rotten egg or skunky smells and tastes to beer.

To Avoid

Establish and maintain sanitary and sterile brewing conditions. Maintain proper fermentation temperatures.

VEGETABLE (COOKED)

Off Flavor

Flavor of cooked corn, cabbage, broccoli, or other vegetables. This smell is not to be confused with the smells or tastes of rotten vegetables (oxidation) or raw vegetables (a desired quality of some hops).

Source

The cooked-vegetable off flavor found in beer is actually a combination of two separate off flavors, sulfurlike (hydrogen sulfide and larger sulfur-containing molecules) and dimethyl-sulfide (DMS). The combination of the "rotten egg" hydrogen sulfide and the "sweet, cornlike" DMS produces a sour/sweet flavor reminiscent of certain cooked vegetables. Bacterial contamination is almost certainly to blame when both off flavors are found in beer, since the same bacteria that produce excess hydrogen sulfide often produce excess DMS as well.

To Avoid

Establish and maintain sanitary and sterile brewing conditions.

YEASTY

Off Flavor

Excessive and harsh — sometimes astringent — taste of yeast often having a slight sulfury flavor.

Source

Large amounts of dead yeast, which have, in essence, digested themselves, releasing bitter resins, lipids, and nitrogen and sulfur-containing molecules.

To Avoid

Use high-quality yeast in good condition. Use proper siphoning or decanting techniques to remove a majority of wort yeast during **racking** and/or bottling.

Off Flavor Identification Aids

To help identify off flavors in your own or someone else's beer, you can use two identification aids provided here. The first is the American Society of Brewing Chemists' flavor wheel, an amazing tool to help the inexperienced and even experienced homebrewer identify specific beer problems (see page 84).

Using the Flavor Wheel

The flavor wheel has three separate (but related) circles. The innermost circle divides all beer characteristics into either *taste* or *odor*. The next circle breaks these two categories into broad taste or aroma descriptions. For instance, *mouthfeel*, *bitter*, and *sulfury*. Finally, the outer wheel contains descriptors of beer off flavor. Note that separate but related problems appear close together such as *acetylaldehyde* (remember that's the smell of little green apples) and *fruity*.

To use the flavor wheel, we first find the smell or off flavor that we have detected in our beer. Let's say we smelled something like *cooked vegetables* in our beer. We find this problem on the outer circle of the flavor wheel and discover that this is a *sulfury* off flavor. We go one more step in and find that it is characterized as an *odor* problem.

Perhaps a more practical example is seen by using the flavor wheel in reverse, working from the general to the more specific. Let's say you smelled something bad in your beer. A quick look at the flavor wheel shows that *odors* fall into about eight categories from *oxidized-stale-musty* on one end all the way to the category *aromatic-fragrant-fruity-floral* on the other end. You reevaluate the smell, considering each of the possible categories of odors, and decide that it is *sulfury*. Looking at the flavor wheel, we see that *sulfury* off odors can be *yeasty* to simply *sulfury* with some variations in between. We consider this range and decide that the odor is that of *cooked vegetable*. Turning to page 82 we are reminded that a *cooked vegetable* off odor is actually a combination of a sulfury and a DMS problem. Often this problem is caused by

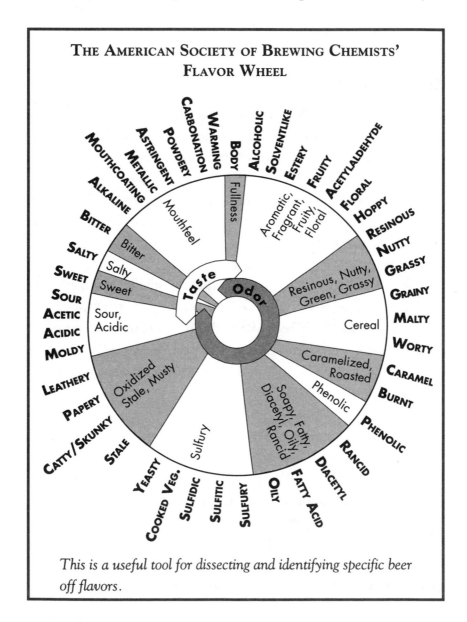

THE AMERICAN SOCIETY OF BREWING CHEMISTS'
FLAVOR WHEEL

This is a useful tool for dissecting and identifying specific beer off flavors.

bacterial infection. We now know both the specific off flavor and the probable cause and can change our brewing method to eliminate this problem.

Other problems, both *taste* and *odor,* can be diagnosed using a similar method. The flavor wheel lets the homebrewer work logically through the possibilities to pinpoint the specific source of the problem.

The second off-flavor identification aid compiles all the off flavors in an easy-reference table (next two pages). To use this table, look for the particular smell or taste you notice in a beer in the left-hand column. The corresponding category in the right-hand column identifies the problem. Now that you know the problem, you can read up on it by referring to the specific entry earlier in this chapter.

Easy-Reference Guide to Identifying Off Flavors

Specific Taste or Odor	Off Flavor (See pages 58 to 82)
Acetic-cider	Acetylaldehyde
Acetone	Alcoholic/Solventlike
Adhesive bandage strip	Phenolic/Medicinal
Apple	Fruity/Estery
Baby diapers	Oxidation
Banana	Fruity/Estery
Banana/rose	Alcoholic/Solventlike
Bloodlike	Metallic
Bready aroma	Acetylaldehyde
Burning match	Hydrogen Sulfide/Sulfurlike
Butter (rancid)	Diacetyl
Butterscotch	Diacetyl
Cloudy	Haze (Chill/Permanent)
Clovelike	Phenolic/Medicinal
Coinlike	Metallic
Cooked corn	Vegetable (cooked)
Cooked celery	Vegetable (cooked)
Cooked parsnip	Vegetable (cooked)
Cooked vegetable, other	Vegetable (cooked)
Drying	Astringent
Electrical fire	Phenolic/Medicinal
Freshly cut grass smell	Grassy
Fruits (other than specific)	Fruity/Estery
Green apples	Acetylaldehyde
Hop taste or aroma inappropriate for style	Hoppy
Hot or spicy flavors	Alcoholic/Solventlike
Iron, tin (or other metals)	Metallic
Lacquer thinner	Alcoholic/Solventlike
Lemon	Sour/Acidic (rear sides of tongue)
Listerine	Phenolic/Medicinal
Medicine chest	Phenolic/Medicinal

Specific Taste or Odor	Off Flavor (See pages 58 to 82)
Metallic/powdery coating in mouth	Astringent
Nutty	Oxidation
Paper	Oxidation
Pear	Fruity/Estery
Pineapple	Oxidation
Plastic	Chlorophenols or Phenolic/Medicinal
Puckering	Astringent
Raspberry	Fruity/Estery
Raw grain taste	Husky/Grainy
Rotten eggs	Hydrogen Sulfide/Sulfurlike
Rotten vegetables	Oxidation
Salt/ion taste (see table on page 15)	Salty (front sides of tongue)
Shellfish (e.g., oysters)	Vegetable (cooked)
Sherry	Oxidation
Skunk aroma	Light-Struck/Skunky (known as "Catty" in England)
Slickness on tongue	Diacetyl
Slight sulfur taste	Yeasty
Smoky	Phenolic/Medicinal
Sour	Sour/Acidic (rear sides of tongue)
Strawberry	Fruity/Estery
Sweet, cooked corn	Dimethyl Sulfide (DMS)
Table salt	Salty (front sides of tongue)
Tart	Astringent or Sour/Acidic (rear sides of tongue)
Tomato plants	Oxidation
Vinegar	Sour/Acidic (rear sides of tongue) or Astringent
Warming effect in mouth	Alcoholic/Solventlike
Wet cardboard	Oxidation
Winey	Oxidation
Yeast flavor (excessive and harsh)	Yeasty

6. Evaluating Beer

If you're reading this book, presumably you're more than remotely interested in being able to tell what makes a good beer good and a bad beer bad. This feat requires a knowledge base, training in how to properly taste and evaluate a beer, and experience in applying both.

Adding to Your Knowledge Base

At this point you are well on your way to understanding the basic chemistry and biochemistry of beer. Now you need to couple your book knowledge with real-world applications such as knowing the what, when, and how of tasting a beer. What does malt taste like? Can you tell the difference between aromatic, flavoring, and bittering hops? How much is too much malt or hops? How do you assess specialty flavors and aromas? How should all of these things combine in each style of beer? With a little effort anyone can become skilled at answering these questions.

In a nutshell, you are simply smelling, looking at, and tasting a beer and deciding if certain qualities required by the style are present and certain off flavors are absent. All of the good tastes are probably already in your beer-tasting repertoire — malty aroma and sweetness, hop aromas and bitterness, and a few specialty tastes. The off flavors are rather simple to pick up, too, given a good description and a little practice. If you don't yet know what causes a beer to smell like adhesive bandage strips versus baby diapers, don't worry — just keep a copy of this book handy, with Chapter 5 carefully earmarked.

One of the best places to begin increasing your knowledge is with the official beer-style categories. In the United States, the American Homebrewers Association (AHA) sets the standard style guidelines, which include alcohol percentage, hop bitterness range (given in International Bittering Units or IBU) and color (given in Standard Reference Method units or SRM). Get an up-to-date copy of these guidelines from your local homebrew supply shop, the entry packet of a homebrew competition, or in issues of the AHA publication *Zymurgy*. You probably don't have to memorize all the style standards and, besides, they usually change a bit from year to year. Just get a good feeling of the predominate characteristics of each style. You may also want to read through Papazian's *The New Complete Joy of Home Brewing* to get more of a down-to-earth description of what characteristics make a style. With either of these style description resources, and your trusty copy of *Brew Chem 101*, competent evaluation of beer becomes quite easy.

How to Taste Beer

Hopefully we have our knowledge base down, but what about the next question? How should one properly evaluate a beer? First of all, remember that there are two major categories of beer — lagers and ales — as discussed in Chapter 1. Lagers, in general, have cleaner aromas and flavors. Ales, on the other hand, have more complexities, especially what is called "fruitiness" due to extra esters. Second, realize that good beer is not one-dimensional, but rather a mixture of tastes, aromas, and feelings. The differing mixture of these qualities is what gives us the wide range of beer styles. In particular, a tasting of beer can almost always be broken down into a beginning, a middle, and an end. We'll talk about this more in the **"Tasting"** section on page 93. Finally, realize that beer, like good food, should be savored by all the senses, including look, smell, taste, feeling, and, yes, even sound. We'll see how next.

A fairly standard method of reviewing the qualities of a beer is used by experienced beer drinkers around the world and forms the basis for evaluation during competitive judging. In agreement with this standard method, I follow a standard protocol of **prepouring, pouring, smelling, looking,** and **tasting.**

Prepouring

For bottled beer you can do an initial assessment of a few potential problems even before you've popped the cap. First check the liquid level in the bottle. Bottle-fill levels less than 1"± ½" (2.54 cm ± 1.27 cm) below the cap may produce oxidation off flavors and decrease the carbonation level. Bottles filled almost to the top may produce over-carbonated beer, as well as metallic off flavors if the beer has interacted much with an uncoated metal cap. Also, green or clear bottles may lead to a light-struck/skunky off smell. Now pop the cap and listen for the pitch of the gas release. (I told you sound would play a part!) High pitches usually mean high carbonation; low pitches, low carbonation. You'll be able to verify any of these potential problems later, so just mentally note them and move on.

Pouring

First of all, if the beer is in a bottle, get a glass, preferably one with a wide top (your best bet is a standard pint beer glass). The quarter-sized hole in the top of a bottle really won't let you smell or taste anything. Don't pour beer down the side of the glass. Hold the bottle a few inches (about 5 cm) above the glass and pour down into the middle of the glass, so aromas can be released. As you pour, note the size and fullness of the head. You'll actually check the head retention a bit later, but now is the time to get a reference point.

Smelling

Once the beer is poured, pick it up right away and smell it. A lot of people look at the color and clarity at this point, but, meanwhile, all the nice aromas are escaping. Why miss some of the best parts of a beer? The colors will be the same as when the beer was poured; the smell may not. So, smell first. When you smell a beer, really smell it. Put your nose in the glass and take a good whiff. You're trying to get a measure of the malt and hops aromas and any specialty smells that are appropriate to the style. Those smells are at their best at this point, so pick them up and note them. You may also pick up some important off smells (such as corny-sweet, adhesive bandage strip, solventlike, baby diapers, or cardboard). It will take 15 to 30 seconds for your nose to clear after the first good whiff, so take a break and think about what you smelled. When you're through, take another good smell to double-check or verify your conclusions.

Looking

Now's the time to pretend you're a wine judge and do the "look at the clarity and color" thing. Is the color right for the style?

Compare it with the description and the Standard Reference Method (SRM) number in the AHA guidelines. As examples, water is 0 SRM; straw/gold pilsners (such as Budweiser or Pilsner Urquell) are 1.0 to 5.5 SRM; amber beers run between 5.5 and 18; Bass Pale Ale is a light to pale amber at 10 SRM; Michelob Classic Dark, a darker amber beer, is considered to be exactly 17 SRM; dark amber or copper beers run between 18 and 26; dark or black beers are 26 to 40 and over; and stouts, such as Guinness, have an SRM of 35 or higher and are considered black beers.

Check the clarity, as well. You may have to find a bright light and tilt the glass a fair amount to be able to see through darker beers. Be sure to wipe off any condensation on the glass. If you're judging wheat styles, keep in mind that they're supposed to be cloudy.

Finally, check the apparent carbonation and head retention. Remember what the head looked like at first pouring? Is it still there?

Tasting

Before you start tasting, you need to learn about "taste profiles." As mentioned earlier, the taste of beer includes a *beginning, middle,* and *end* that together make up the "taste profile." Understanding each part of this profile will dramatically increase your appreciation for the beer you drink and greatly aid your ability to accurately evaluate it.

The *beginning* is the first taste that hits your mouth (and tongue) and is usually associated with the sweet tastes of malt. Some styles will have very strong, long-lasting malt starts while others will have weak, short ones. There will always be some malt taste, since beer is a malted beverage. Sweet off flavors like dimethyl sulfide (DMS) or diacetyl will also be noticeable at the beginning of a beer taste.

The *middle* is when specialty tastes often emerge such as fruit flavors, toasted or roasted grains, flavoring hops, and so on. Sometimes the beginning malt taste will have faded and sometimes it will still be detectable. In a style without a specialty taste, the middle provides a transitional stage leading to the finish. If this is the case, the transition should be smooth. (This is discussed in more detail on page 95 in the talk about balance and conditioning.)

Finally, we come to the *end,* or finish, of a beer's taste profile. This is where you'll find — what else? — the finishing hops. Specialty flavors are often still present, especially fruit and toasted/roasted grains. Usually any malt flavors are gone at this point. The end or finish of a beer can be short or long, lingering or ending clean.

As you're working through all stages of the taste profile, consider the beer's body. This quality is pretty self-explanatory. The important thing is to be sure the style you're judging has the body it's supposed to have. Check the official style description to be sure.

Distinguishing Flavors

At this point, you're probably sick and tired of all this work and thinking, "I wish I wasn't judging and could just sit back and taste it for pure, unadulterated enjoyment." Well, that's exactly what your first taste should be. Don't worry about chemicals or reactions now, just take a taste, swish it around your mouth, and get an initial and overall impression of the beer. Take another taste and start dissecting the beer, including the three parts of the taste profile, as discussed under "Tasting." Get the beer all through your mouth and over your tongue. Different parts of your tongue pick up different kinds of flavors (see illustration on page 96). For instance, if the beer you're tasting is supposed to be sweet, pay attention to the tip of your tongue. If it's supposed to be hoppy, focus on the back-middle of your tongue. Think about the various off flavors and see if you pick any of them up. Be aware of combination flavors. For example, overly roasted or burnt grains in stouts can give both bitter and sour tastes, so be conscious of any combination flavors that may be present in a particular style.

You should also evaluate **balance, conditioning**, and **aftertaste**. Balance refers to a correct ratio of malt, hops, and specialty tastes and aromas per the style. This gets a bit subjective, but it helps if you concentrate on what the beer is supposed to taste like and if, in fact, all the flavors are blending together to give you an appropriate and enjoyable drinking experience. Conditioning refers to whether or not the beer's age — young, just right, or too old. Young beers tend to have stronger and more separate flavors that don't quite blend. Older beers are often filled with cardboardy, stale flavors of oxidation. Nicely conditioned beers lead the drinker through a smooth transition of the style's correct flavors from start to finish. Conditioning can also be roughly determined by the size of the bubbles in the head — small bubbles mean it's too young, huge ones indicate it's too old, and somewhere in the middle is just right — but I put more weight on the taste assessment. Aftertastes in certain styles of beer are not only acceptable, but required. A style like an India pale ale with a strong hops finish should have just that — a strong hops finish that stays with you for a while. Beer styles that should end "clean" should leave the mouth empty and refreshed, but not wanting.

The illustration of the tongue will help you learn to distinguish the flavors and/or off flavors you may be tasting, depending on what you're experiencing on your tongue. When you're tasting a beer, think about which part of the tongue you are feeling and why. Once you develop this awareness, you'll be able to easily differentiate many basic and even combination tastes.

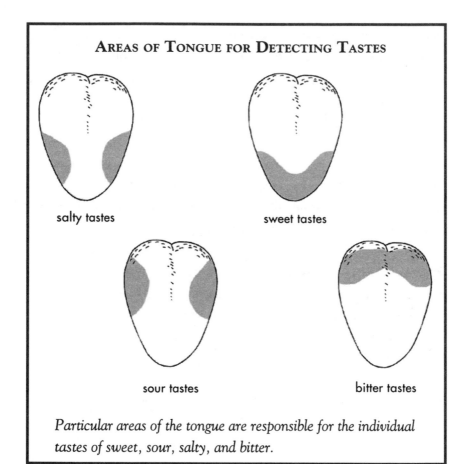

AREAS OF TONGUE FOR DETECTING TASTES

salty tastes

sweet tastes

sour tastes

bitter tastes

Particular areas of the tongue are responsible for the individual tastes of sweet, sour, salty, and bitter.

Gaining Judging Experience

Beer drinking and judging experience can't be taught in a book, but fortunately, it is not hard work! This required practice can be achieved by two basic methods: Drink a lot of beer at your local tavern or taste each batch of your friend's and your own homebrew. However, chances are you'll only pick up bits and pieces of experience over a relatively long period of time. A far better, easier, and, to many, a more enjoyable way to gain both experience and a more complete understanding of homebrewing (both good and bad) is to learn to formally or semiformally judge your own and others' brews and to apply these abilities in an organized manner. If you do your practice judging in an organized fashion, you'll also soon pick up minor variations in taste and pick up off flavors that would otherwise be missed. Additionally, you will almost certainly be exposed to some new and different styles and/or flavors of beer while judging homebrew, thereby expanding your brewing and tasting horizons. Some possible ways of doing "organized" judging include:

* Go to your favorite beer bar and try just a few beers of the same style. Try to pick out the defining characteristics of each as well as any off flavors.
* Throw a beer-tasting party with carefully selected beers and discuss the characteristics of each beer.
* Challenge your homebrewing buddies to all make the same style of beer. When they're ready, get everyone together, discuss each beer, and pick a "homebrew champ."
* Judge a local homebrew competition. They're always looking for new judges (experience not necessary). See below for more information.

In formal and even semiformal judging, don't just think about what you're smelling and tasting, but also why and how it smells or tastes that way. You may also want to write those reasons down, thereby solidifying your thought processes. In doing so, all those little bits of knowledge you've acquired about brewing technique will be brought together, applied, and even increased with respect to a real-world case.

If you're interested in really formal judging, consider volunteering as a judge or steward at a local homebrew competition. Although anyone can judge at official competitions, those people who have passed the Beer Judge Certification Program (BJCP) are, for the most part, better and much more sought after. Examinations are given several times a year at some of the larger homebrewing competitions. You can find out more about the program from your local homebrew club, homebrew shop, or the American Homebrewers Association, P.O. Box 1679, Boulder, CO 80306-1679, Phone (303) 447-0816.

Finally, please remember that beer contains alcohol, and no matter how big or tough you are, the alcohol *will* affect you. Practice responsible and safe, organized judgings for both yourself and any guests.

Glossary

Adjunct. Any additional ingredient to beer besides water, malted grain, hops, and yeast. A common adjunct is unmalted specialty grains, which may offer special flavors and coloring to beer.

Ale. Major type of beer with a characteristic fuller body and complex, usually "fruity" flavors. Ales are fermented at 50 to 75°F. *See also* **Lager**.

All-Grain. Method of brewing in which the equivalent of *extract* is prepared from grains by the homebrewer instead of by a commercial company. All-grain brewing provides the homebrewer the most flexibility and control over beer tastes and character and is the least expensive versus other brewing methods. As a rule, commercial breweries, microbreweries, and brewpubs use the all-grain method.

Alpha Acid. A type of soft resin in the hop plant that is absorbed by the wort during boiling and provides the primary bitterness to beer. Alpha acid content is reported for each hop crop as a percentage of the total weight of the hop cone.

Amylopectin. A type of starch consisting of long strings *and* branched individual sugar molecules. *See also* **Amylose** and **Starch**.

Amylose. A type of starch consisting of long, straight strings of individual sugar molecules. Amylose does not have any sugar branches. *See also* **Amylopectin** and **Starch**.

Aromatic (Finishing) Hops. Hops used in a beer recipe to give hop aromas by short periods of addition to the boiling wort. Aromatic hops are often noble hop types due to the pleasant and strong aromas of these varieties. Aromatic hops should never be boiled longer than 1 to 2 minutes or the aromatic molecules will be lost; for this reason they are often referred to as "finishing" hops.

Attenuation. A measure of the amount of sugar in the wort that has been converted to ethanol and carbon dioxide. Attenuation is measured by the drop in specific gravity using a **hydrometer** or **sarchometer**. The rate and amount of attenuation is characteristic of each yeast strain.

Barley. The grain of the cereal plant *Hordeum vulgare* used as the primary source of fermentable sugars and of proteins and other flavor molecules in beer.

Bittering (Boiling) Hops. Hops used in a beer recipe to give primary hop bitterness to beer by long periods of addition to the boiling wort (30 to 60 minutes). Due to the duration of time in the wort, these hops are often referred to as "boiling" hops.

Bittering Units. Unit of measure of level of bitterness added to the wort during the boil. Calculation of bittering units allows easy changes in amount and variety of hops while still obtaining the same bitterness level. Bittering units are defined as the *amount of hops (ounces)* × *alpha-acid content (percent)*. Also known as Home Bittering Units.

Blow-off Tube. Device used in place of a *fermentation lock (bubbler)* during the first three to six days of primary fermentation to allow escape of unwanted hops and wort oils that would otherwise remain in the beer.

Bottle Age. Period of time after bottling or non-carbonated kegging in which carbonation and head form due to the fermentation of *priming sugar*. Bottle aging usually lasts one to three weeks (sometimes longer for lagers), depending on temperature and yeast variability.

Carboy. Common name for the fermentation vessel, usually made of glass or plastic.

Cold Break. Process by which large proteins and polyphenol molecules fall out of the wort (precipitate) during wort cooling and fermentation. Cold break helps to eliminate molecules that would otherwise cause haze and cloudiness. Fast wort cooling causes a more efficient cold break.

Dry Hopping. Hops used after wort boiling to provide hop aromatic flavors. Dry hopping provides more aromatics than aromatic (finishing) hops since the hop oils are never exposed to boiling water.

Enzyme. A protein molecule that performs a biochemical reaction. Brewers are usually concerned about enzymes that cut apart proteins or sugars.

Extract. Concentrated solution of sugars and proteins derived from mashing. Extract is concentrated by removal of most of the water from the mash (liquid extract) or all of the water (dry extract). Dry extracts provide about 1¼ to 1½ times the fermentable sugar content as liquid extracts. Recipes should be adjusted accordingly when switching between the two types.

Fermentation. The biochemical process by which yeast converts sugar molecules into one molecule of carbon dioxide (CO_2) and one molecule of ethanol (alcohol). The process of fermentation takes place without oxygen and is, therefore, called *anaerobic*.

Fermentation Lock (Bubbler). Device used to seal fermentation vessel from outside air but still allow the release of carbon dioxide produced during fermentation. Fermentation locks usually rely on water to create this seal. As carbon dioxide escapes, bubbles form, leading to the common name.

Flavoring Hops. Hops used to give clean, crisp, hop flavor instead of bitterness (from bittering hops) or hop aromas (from aromatic hops). Flavoring hops are added to the boiling wort for at least 10, but no longer than 15, minutes.

Flocculation. A measure of the amount of large protein molecules and yeast cells that stick together and fall (precipitate) out of the beer. The rate and amount of flocculation is characteristic of each yeast strain.

Grist. Crushed malt grains used for mashing. Grist should be only gently crushed to expose the husk interior, not broken apart or ground into powder. Ground grains will result in tannins and astringency in beer.

High-Alpha Hops. Hops with a relatively large percentage of alpha-acid bittering resins, roughly 6 to 10 percent. *See also* **Super-Alpha Hops**.

Hops. Flowers of the female hop plant *Humulus lupulus*, originally used as a preservative for beer. Hops provide primary bitterness to beer as well as aroma and other flavors. A wide variety of hops are available, each offering its own bitterness and flavor characteristics.

Hops Schedule. Recipe of type and amount of hops added to wort along with total time in boiling wort, which defines the hop flavors and aromas for that beer. A hops schedule often includes addition of **Bittering Hops**, **Flavoring Hops**, and **Aromatic Hops**.

Hot Break. Process by which large proteins and other molecules fall (precipitate) out of the wort during wort boiling. Hot break helps to eliminate molecules that would otherwise cause haze and cloudiness.

Hydrometer (Sarchometer). Device used to measure the amount of sugars in the wort that could be converted to alcohol.

Ion. A charged atom or small molecule that creates certain chemical, biochemical, or biological characteristics in beer.

Krausen. The foamy white residue topped with a scummy brown residue containing very bitter "fusel" oils. The krausen forms during the initial stages (first three to six days) of primary fermentation. The krausen and bitter oils will fall back into the beer, causing mild off flavors unless removed (sterilely) by a blow-off tube or by manually collecting and removing the krausen (krausening).

Lager. From the German word meaning "to store." Major type of beer with a characteristic light body and clean, crisp flavors. Lagers are fermented at 35 to 50°F and, as the name implies, stored or aged for a certain period of time at similar temperatures. *See also* **Ale**.

Mash/Mashing. The process by which proteins and sugars are extracted from malted barley. Mashing involves a series of steps involving temperature, pH, and enzymatic changes to provide the optimal conditions for this extraction.

Noble Hops. Specific hop varieties high in the hop oil humulene, known for their contribution of "elegant" hop aroma to certain beer styles. Noble hop varieties include Fuggle, Golding, Hallertau, Hersbruck, Saaz, Spalt, Styrian, and Tettnanger.

Off Flavors. General term for any number of unwanted flavors or aromas in beer, indicative of an error in brewing technique. Defining off flavors must be done with care and knowledge since some beer styles or brands are typified by what would normally be considered an off flavor.

Pitch/Pitching. Term used to describe the addition of something to the wort or beer. Pitching almost always refers to the addition of yeast to the cooled wort.

Priming Sugar. Sugar added to fermented wort, which will provide carbonation to beer. Exactly ¾ cup (177.75 ml) of corn sugar is normally used before bottling for 5 gallons (18.9 liters) of beer. To achieve carbonation with smaller bubbles, resulting in a smoother head, 1¼ cup (296.25 ml) of dry malt extract can be used. Priming sugar can also be provided by means of unfermented, sterile wort or other simple, fermentable sugars. Deviation by unpracticed hands from standard amounts and types of priming sugar can easily cause over- or under-carbonated beer.

Racking. The process by which beer (fermented or unfermented) is transferred from one vessel to another. Racking is commonly done from a primary to a secondary fermenter or just before bottling.

Raffinose. Complex sugar composed of two glucose and one fructose molecules. Although not a major component of beer wort, raffinose is used to biochemically define lager and ale yeast. Lager yeast completely process raffinose; ale yeast leave a residual G—G sugar, known as *melibiose*.

Single-Stage Fermentation. Fermentation schedule that allows beer to fully ferment in only one carboy followed by bottling or kegging.

Sparge/Sparging. Term describing the collection of unfermented wort by the removal of malt grains. Sparging is usually used to describe the controlled filtration of water through mashed grains to collect the unfermented sugars and proteins. Sparging can also be used to refer to any general collection of liquid wort by the simple removal of particulates (e.g., filtering spent hops and malt grains from the wort after boiling).

Starch. Complex branched chain of from 25 to more than 1000 glucose residues. Starch is often used as a general term for all large glucose sugars (*amylose*, *amylopectin*, and true *starch*). This usage is, in strict biochemical terms, incorrect.

Super-Alpha Hops. Hops with a very high percentage of alpha-acid bittering resins, usually over 10 percent. *See also* **High-Alpha Hops**.

Trub. (pronounced *troob*) The whitish, scummy layer that forms on the bottom of fermenting wort containing precipitated proteins, dead or dying yeast cells, lipids and fats, and other molecules. If beer is not removed from contact with the trub after two to three weeks, off flavors can develop.

Two-Stage Fermentation. Fermentation schedule that requires a second carboy for a second stage of beer fermentation. Two-stage fermentation is usually only valuable for beers that must ferment for an extended period of time (greater than two to three weeks) and offers removal of the beer from the potentially damaging trub. Lagers should always be removed from the trub for their aging period.

Wort. (pronounced *wert*) Unfermented beer, consisting of malt, hops, and any adjuncts, before yeast addition (*pitching*).

Further Reading

Brewing Techniques. Box 322, Eugene, OR 97403. 1-800-427-2993.

A new magazine on the brewing scene that has received its share of praise for detailed but easily understood articles on a multitude of brewing topics. For the brewer interested in the technical side of the craft, this periodical is highly recommended.

Beaumont, Stephen. *A Taste for Beer.* Pownal, VT: Storey Communications, Inc., 1995.

An interesting and rather novel work discussing the more social aspects of beer and beer drinking. Beaumont shows how beer can be properly matched to seasons, food, and events. A collection of recipes made with beer makes this book a unique addition to your brewing bookshelf.

Eckhardt, Fred. *The Essentials of Beer Style.* Portland, OR: Fred Eckhardt Associates, 1989.

An excellent book describing in some detail beer styles of the world. An important reference for both the experienced and inexperienced homebrewer.

Brewer's Publications, ed., *Evaluating Beer.* Boulder, CO: Brewers Publications, 1993.

A collection of articles by leading authorities on beer judging and evaluation. Chapters provide a somewhat intense discussion of very specific aspects of beer judging and may be too focused for the general reader.

Fix, George. *Principles of Brewing Science.* (M. Raizman, ed.). Boulder, CO: Brewers Publications, 1989.

An advanced and in-depth review of brewing chemistry and biochemistry. Some knowledge of chemistry and biochemistry is suggested for the reader.

Fix, G. J., et al. "A Homebrewer's Guide to Beer Flavor Descriptors." *Zymurgy.* 10: 33–53, 1987.

An excellent review by some of the leading authorities on homebrewing covering a large number of brewing off flavors and outlining their causes and methods to avoid them. Available for a nominal price from the Association of Home Brewers, P.O. Box 1510, Boulder, CO 80306-1510, Phone (303) 546-6514.

Jackson, Michael. *The Simon & Schuster Pocket Guide to Beer.* New York: Simon & Schuster, 1988.

Not a technical manual, but an unsurpassed book for the traveling beer drinker. Small enough to fit in your pocket, but big enough to tell you where to go for a good beer anywhere in the world.

―――. *The New World Guide to Beer.* Philadelphia: The Running Press, 1988.

The leading authority on beers of the world shares his tasting experience and vast knowledge of beer.

Miller, Dave. *Dave Miller's Homebrewing Guide.* Pownal, VT: Storey Communications, 1995.

If you're looking for a standard brewing technique book with a lot of detail, this is it. Dave Miller conveys his experience in homebrewing to the reader in an easily read and understood style.

Noonan, Gregory J. *Brewing Lager Beer.* Boulder, CO: Brewers Publications, 1986.

Focusing on lager beer, this book will lead the serious, semiexperienced homebrewer into the experienced category. As the back of the book warns, though, this book is for only intermediate, expert, or professional brewers.

Papazian, Charlie. *The New Complete Joy of Homebrewing.* Boulder, CO: Brewers Publications, 1991.

Many people refer to this amazing compendium as "the Bible of homebrewing," and I'm not going to disagree. Although some details found in Miller, Noonan, or Fix are lacking, this book is the first book to own if you are a beginning to experienced brewer.

Zymurgy. American Homebrewers Association, P.O. Box 1679, Boulder, CO 80306-1679.

The original magazine for homebrewers, an excellent publication to keep you in touch with all in the world of brewing.

Index

Italic page numbers = Illustrations
Boldface page numbers = tables/charts